Denis Brenan Bullen (1802–66), Inspector of Anatomy for the Province of Munster

Maynooth Studies in Local History

SERIES EDITOR Raymond Gillespie

This volume is one of five short books published in the Maynooth Studies in Local History series in 2021. Like their predecessors they range widely over the local experience in the Irish past. Chronologically they range across the 19th century and into the 20th century but they focus on problems that reappeared in almost every period of Irish history. They chronicle the experiences of individuals grappling with their world from the Cork surgeon, Denis Brenan Bullen, in the early 19th century to the politician and GAA administrator Peadar Cowan in the 20th century. From a different perspective they resurrect whole societies under stress from the rural tensions in Knock, Co. Mayo, to the impact of the Famine on Sir William Palmer's estates in Mayo. A rather different sort of institution under stress, Dublin's cattle market, provides the framework for charting the final years of the world that depended on that institution. Geographically they range across the length of the country from Dublin to Cork and westwards into Mayo. Socially they move from those living on the margins of society in Knock through to the prosperous world of the social elite in Cork. In doing so they reveal diverse and complicated societies that created the local past and present the range of possibilities open to anyone interested in studying that past. Those possibilities involve the dissection of the local experience in the complex and contested social worlds of which it is part as people strove to preserve and enhance their positions within their local societies. It also reveals the forces that made for cohesion in local communities and those that drove people apart, whether through large scale rebellion or through acts of inter-personal violence. Such studies of local worlds over such long periods are vital for the future since they not only stretch the historical imagination but provide a longer perspective on the evolution of society in Ireland and help us to understand more fully the complex evolution of the Irish experience. These works do not simply chronicle events relating to an area within administrative or geographically determined boundaries, but open the possibility of understanding how and why particular regions had their own personality in the past. Such an exercise is clearly one of the most exciting challenges for the future and demonstrates the vitality of the study of local history in Ireland.

Like their predecessors, these five short books are reconstructions of the socially diverse worlds of the poor as well as the rich, women as well as men, the geographical marginal of Mayo as well as those located near the centre of power. They reconstruct the way in which those who inhabited those worlds lived their daily lives, often little affected by the large themes that dominate the writing of national history. In addressing these issues, studies such as those presented in these short books, together with their predecessors, are at the forefront of Irish historical research and represent some of the most innovative and exciting work being undertaken in Irish history today. They also provide models that others can follow up and adapt in their own studies of the Irish past. In such ways will we understand better the regional diversity of Ireland and the social and cultural basis for that diversity. They, with their predecessors, convey the vibrancy and excitement of the world of Irish local history today.

Maynooth Studies in Local History: Number 150

Denis Brenan Bullen (1802–66), Inspector of Anatomy for the Province of Munster

The controversial career of a Cork surgeon

Michael V. Hanna

FOUR COURTS PRESS

Set in 10pt on 12pt Bembo by
Carrigboy Typesetting Services for
FOUR COURTS PRESS LTD
7 Malpas Street, Dublin 8, Ireland
www.fourcourtspress.ie
and in North America for
FOUR COURTS PRESS
c/o IPG, 814 N Franklin St, Chicago, IL 60610

ISBN 978–1–84682–969–7

Printed in Ireland
by SprintPrint, Dublin.

Contents

Acknowledgments

I would like to thank the staff of the Department of History, University College Cork (UCC), for instituting the MA in Local History and to recommend it to others. This work is based on the dissertation for that degree. I wish to extend my thanks to Dr Andrew McCarthy, my supervisor, whose continued advice has been of enormous help. The UCC Library, and particularly Mary Lombard and her colleagues in Special Collections, were of tremendous assistance in tracking down primary sources in their wonderful collections. Brian McGee in Cork City Archives provided much help with access to the records of the Cork Workhouse and the Committee of Merchants, and Cork City Library was a valuable source for Cork newspapers. Thanks are also due to Brian Donnelly and staff of the National Archives of Ireland for help in navigating the Chief Secretary's Office papers. I would like to thank Margaret O'Connor for sharing with me her minute book and papers of the Cork County and City Medical and Surgical Society and Honor de Pencier for her certificates of George Russell Dartnell. Grateful thanks are also due to Helen Donovan, Chief Executive Officer of the South Infirmary/Victoria Hospital, for letting me know of, and giving me free access to, a recently discovered cache of old minute books of the South Infirmary dating back to its establishment in 1762. This has enabled us to put an exact date on John Woodroffe's arrival there as 'third surgeon' in 1813. Finally, I would like to thank Timmy O'Connor and Catriona Mulcahy of University Archives, UCC, and the staff of Trinity College Manuscripts Room and Early Printed Books for their invaluable assistance. This work is dedicated to Davis Coakley, who first awakened my interest in medical history.

Introduction

Denis Brenan Bullen was an important figure in the history of medical education in 19th-century Cork. He was secretary and founder member of the Provincial Colleges Committee that worked to bring what would become Queen's College Cork to the city in 1845 and was its first Professor of Surgery. He became the city's *de facto* spokesperson for medicine and medical education matters, providing evidence to various parliamentary select committees. He was the conduit for a major philanthropic gift which he used to reinvigorate and expand the ailing North Charitable Infirmary in 1831. He became Inspector of Anatomy for the Province of Munster after the passing of the Anatomy Act in 1832. He was never far from controversy, and controversy would eventually subsume him and his career. When that career is taken as a whole, it reads something like a Shakespearean tragedy, and in many respects that is what it was; nevertheless, out of the life and career of Denis Brenan Bullen we get a vivid picture of the development of medical education in the city of Cork in the 19th century. His behaviour in a famous medical dispute in 1820, when he was only 17 or 18 years old, set him on the road of a tempestuous career.

In 1820 the cognoscenti of Cork's coffee houses and salons were captivated by a row that blew up between two of the city's foremost medical gentlemen. Normally such rivalries were kept private, within 'the freemasonry of the profession' as Denis Bullen would later describe it to a parliamentary select committee. But this row was conducted publically through three pamphlets, the first from William Bullen, a reply from John Woodroffe and a further reply to Woodroffe from Bullen.

William Bullen was a well-known and well-respected doctor, a pious Catholic with youthful United Irishmen sympathies, apparently long since laid aside, and a reputation for generosity and good works among his Catholic fellow citizens. In 1820 he was elected on to the Board of Trustees of the South Charitable Infirmary – an entirely Protestant body – and thereupon challenged one of the Infirmary's surgeons, John Woodroffe, with professional incompetence in relation to four lithotomy operations conducted on young boys between 1816 and 1818.

John Woodroffe was a Dublin Protestant, son of a wine merchant, whose family had been 17th-century settlers in Bandon and West Carbery. His uncle Samuel had been Precentor of St Fin Barre's Cathedral in Cork in the 1750s. He came to the city as a young military surgeon some time before 1810 when he married Sarah Walsh in Christchurch. In 1811 he began lecturing in Anatomy and in 1813 obtained the position of third surgeon in the South Infirmary.[1] Neil Cronin has described the dispute and the powerful forces that fuelled it in *The medical profession and the exercise of power in early nineteenth-century Cork*.[2] It revolved around the particular case of Patrick Reade, a 16-year-old boy on whom Woodroffe had operated in 1817. Cronin describes lithotomy at this time as 'an iconic operation, requiring the greatest skill and fortitude of the surgeon'.[3]

Denis Brenan Bullen was one of William Bullen's sons, born in 1802, and therefore fifteen or sixteen years old at the time of the operation on Reade. He attended to observe, along with Woodroffe's medical students and army doctors, as was customary at the time, and according to John Woodroffe, he and his brother William, born 1796, who was by that time a young attorney, tutored Patrick Reade and his father to make a formal complaint to the Board of Trustees. Woodroffe produced witnesses who testified that the two young men had visited the Reade home and conspired there to prosecute him for professional incompetence. Denis Bullen was reported to have said to Reade:

> I suppose you would be content with a few pounds, but if Doctor Woodroffe offers you £50 don't take £100, or if he offers you £100, don't take £500 for we will see you righted, but whatever he offers, *get it from under his hand* for then we will begin a lawsuit.

In September 1820, all the physicians and surgeons in Cork were invited, presumably by William Bullen, to an 'open consultation' about the case. Only three attended. One of them, Christopher Bull, was surgeon in ordinary to John Woodroffe at the South Infirmary[4] and was quoted by Denis Bullen as having 'declared the case of Reade a disgrace to [the Infirmary] and all pronounced it to be hopeless and incurable'. According to Woodroffe, Bull solemnly and unequivocally (and perhaps, prudently) denied ever using such expressions.[5]

Denis Brenan Bullen emerges from this, his first entry into a public dispute – and certainly not his last – as a precocious and opinionated young medical student from a Catholic professional background who was prepared to face up to a Protestant surgeon wielding all the levers of power at his command to defend his good name. Bullen went on to live out a controversial if local career as one of Cork's leading medical men.

That career shines a light on the development of medical education in Cork during the 19th century. Having had his first taste of public controversy in 1820, he graduated MD from the University of Edinburgh in 1822 and returned to Cork where one of his earliest gambits was to apply, unsuccessfully, for the post of physician at the Cork Lunatic Asylum, a post that had become vacant on the death of its founder, William Hallaran. He was more successful in 1828 when he was appointed lecturer in Chemistry at the Royal Cork Institution. In 1827 he married Maria Ellen Power and this brought him into contact with Anthony Sampayo, a wealthy Portuguese merchant who had made a large fortune in trade between Cork and Lisbon. Sampayo made a gift of £1,000 to Bullen for charitable purposes and he used this to obtain a surgical post in the North Infirmary and revive its flagging fortunes.

At the end of the 1820s the crimes of William Burke and William Hare[6] led directly to the passing of the Anatomy Act in 1832 which provided for the use by the medical schools of unclaimed bodies from the workhouse. The Anatomy Inspectorate was created to give effect to the Act. Bullen's appointment as Inspector of Anatomy for the Province of Munster was public recognition of his standing in the city. His appointment as Inspector brought him into the centre of Cork's booming medical education business. By 1838 there were three private medical schools in the city and lectures were conducted in the North and South Infirmaries. Bullen estimated there were some 100 medical gentlemen in the city. Of these, at least a quarter taught in these schools and in the two infirmaries. He became secretary and founding member of the Provincial Colleges Committee that led to the founding of Queen's College Cork in 1845. At this stage it seemed that nothing could go wrong for Denis Bullen. He was appointed to the Chair of Surgery in the new college and his son Francis was the first student to register in the new college. One of his colleague professors was Benjamin Alcock, Professor of Anatomy and Physiology. Alcock's arrival in Cork was a turning point in Bullen's fortunes though not immediately so. Ronan O'Rahilly wrote a small monograph on Benjamin Alcock's time in Cork but he appears not to have had access to the Chief Secretary's Official Registered Papers which contain the original correspondence of Bullen, Alcock, Sir Robert Kane, first President of Queen's College Cork, and others. Family history websites have helped in recent months to solve the long running mystery of what happened to Benjamin Alcock after he resigned from Queen's College and emigrated to America.[7] John A. Murphy's history of Queen's / University College Cork (1995) provides a witty and informative account of Cork's university college and is probably the best secondary source for the West Wing fire and its aftermath. The Cork workhouse occupies an important part in Bullen's career, and particularly his clash with Benjamin Alcock, because it was the source of bodies for the medical schools and as Inspector of Anatomy he was responsible for administering the legislation governing their supply. One of his colleagues, Professor Denis Charles O'Connor, spent seventeen years as the infirmary doctor of the Cork workhouse, which he committed to a memoir.[8] Colman O'Mahony has studied the extensive workhouse records providing a clear account of the Famine years.[9]

Bullen's story brings into focus yet another adversary who was proprietor of the Cork School of Medicine on the South Mall, the last private medical school in the city. This was Henry Augustus Caesar, like Bullen a graduate of Edinburgh University but that is where the similarities ended. There are no secondary sources about Caesar except for the briefest mention by Ronan O'Rahilly[10] and a passing reference in John A. Murphy's history of University

College Cork.[11] He applied unsuccessfully for the Chair of Anatomy and Physiology in 1849 and offered to bring his school with him as a dowry when he reapplied in 1854.[12] Caesar was an altogether more wily character than Alcock and his dislike of Bullen was intense. After seeing off Alcock, Bullen tried to close down Caesar's school by withdrawing his licence to practise dissection. A long drawn-out court case ensued that was eventually overtaken by Bullen's disgrace and sacking from Queen's College Cork,[13] and scarcely a year later, by the death of Henry Caesar himself.[14]

Parliamentary papers accessible and searchable on-line provide an essential primary source but the real treasure trove for this study is the Chief Secretary's Office Registered Papers (CSORP) and Chief Secretary's Office Official Papers (CSOOP) in the National Archives of Ireland. Here we find original letters of Denis Bullen, Sir Robert Kane, Benjamin Alcock, William Gardiner (the workhouse medical officer), Samuel Hobart and many more which reveal what was going on beneath the surface. Not all relevant papers are extant; correspondence from Henry Caesar is largely missing, but certain inferences can be drawn from the annotated indexes. 'Treasure trove' is not an exaggeration; the thrill of reading and handling these letters and seeing the comments of the Chief Secretary (always in red ink) brings one back through the centuries to almost touch the anxiety, arrogance, exasperation, outrage and in some cases the Machiavellian cleverness of the protagonists.

1. Early successes

Denis Brenan Bullen was born in 1802 to William Bullen MD and Catherine Quinlan at the family home in Cork's South Parish. His elder brother William was baptized on 25 October 1796 in the presence of his parents and two others – Denis Brenan and Anne Roche. He had at least three sisters, all born after him,[1] but the Bullen family website names seven siblings altogether, one of whom – Mary – died in 1817 after the birth of her first child.[2] It would seem likely that he was named after this Denis Brenan who may have died between the births of the two boys.

His father was a well-known and successful doctor in Cork with a reputation for kindness and generosity among the Catholic poor of the city.[3] In his younger days, he had United Irishman sympathies but these do not seem to have translated into any subversive action that drew attention from the authorities.[4] According to Denis's brother William, Captain Henry Sturgeon, future husband of Sarah Curran, first met his future father-in-law, Joshua Curran, 'at dinner at my father's in Cork' where he earned the old man's 'high admiration'.[5] Daniel O'Connell was another dinner guest during his visits to the Cork Assizes.[6]

His mother 'was regarded with good reason as a saint; her piety and goodness in every relation of life were known to all'.[7] Such evidence enables us to place Bullen in a large, prosperous Catholic family, politically aware, intellectually alive and prepared to give social leadership through professional and religious example. At the same time, their home in the South Mall appears to have been a place where guests of different political and religious views found a welcome.

Bullen was fortunate in being born at the beginning of a golden intellectual age in Cork. Thomas Dix Hincks, Unitarian minister and disciple of Joseph Priestly, arrived in the city in 1790 and immediately began to lecture from his home on Patrick's Hill. In 1803 he founded the Cork Institution, closely modelled on the Royal Institution where Humphrey Davy was drawing large crowds to his Chemistry lectures at this time. Hincks provided lectures in chemistry, natural history, natural philosophy and agriculture.[8] A Royal Charter was obtained in 1807 and an annual government grant of £2,000 placed the Royal Cork Institution on a stable footing. For the next twenty to thirty years it became 'the means of exciting a very general taste for science among the rising young men of the city' and, it would appear, young women too. Several of the lecturers would take pride in the number of ladies attending their lectures.[9] Art and sculpture also found fertile ground among the prosperous and aspiring middle classes of the city. The Canova casts were presented as a gift to the RCI by George IV in 1817. These, together with anatomical lectures and dissections by John Woodroffe – offered *gratis* to young artists – inspired a generation of artists such as Daniel Maclise, William Fisher, Samuel Forde and the sculptor John Hogan.[10]

Woodroffe began lecturing when Denis Bullen was 9 years old. His father was sceptical, possibly even antagonistic, believing that 'no such attempt could ever succeed in this city'– but the time was ripe and it did, and by the time Bullen was 16 years old, it was the only anatomical school in southern Ireland.[11] Woodroffe provided lectures and dissections, boasting that 'the facilities of dissection have been so ample as to give my pupils very superior advantages on that score'.[12] It is not clear if Denis attended Woodroffe's school. He said in later life that he was apprenticed to his father but does not say that this represented the entirety of his pre-university medical education.

Students entering the Army Medical Department were also admitted *gratis* to Woodroffe's school. George Russell Dartnell (1798/9–1878) qualified on both counts. Several years older than Bullen, Dartnell was the third son of John Dartnell and Alice Russell of Rathkeale, Co. Limerick.[13] George began his studies with John Woodroffe in 1814 and spent the next five years as his apprentice in the South Charitable Infirmary. He was one of the 'rising young men of the city' who benefited from attending courses at the RCI in Materia Medica (Dr Sharkey), Medicinal Chemistry (Edmund Davy, cousin of Humphrey), Botany (Mr Thompson) and Natural Philosophy (James Willes, MD). He then spent six months in Dublin at the Richmond Hospital and six months at St George's Hospital in London attending lectures by Sir Everard Home and Charles Bell.[14] These various apprenticeships and lecture courses extended from 1814 to 1822 and were accepted as preparation for his army medical examinations. Dartnell is of interest to us not because of his subsequent distinguished medical career, nor for his remarkable watercolours, but for a detailed account of a student grave-robbing escapade in Cork during his time at Woodroffe's school. Unfortunately we do not have room here to relate it in full but it is available online and is one of the best Irish accounts in the genre. Dartnell recounted the tale over a campfire in the Canadian wilderness to his friend and fellow artist Sir James Alexander in 1843 and it subsequently appeared in volume 1 of Alexander's memoir.[15]

Grave-robbing has left a long legacy in the medical profession. The Anatomy Act was intended to put an end to it but it took decades before it truly ended. It was not so much the Act that brought it to an end but a gradual change in attitude among the public to the point where voluntary donations removed the need for unclaimed bodies of the poor. Nor did it gain for the surgeons the respectability they craved. It simply moved the burden to the sick poor who over the coming decades would die in droves of famine, fever and consumption in the workhouse and the charitable infirmaries. It led to a great fear among the poor that if they entered the workhouse and died there, they would end up on the anatomists' slab and their remains dumped or, to use a phrase borrowed from Dartnell's account, 'reserved for a preparation'. There was a case in 1827 of a poor family burying a deceased family member under the floor of their cabin in the South Liberties of Cork in order to protect it from Woodroffe's students.[16] Its real legacy though was to create a secretive culture in the medical profession and among medical students. This ambiguity in professional and public perceptions of medical educators over the succeeding decades of the 19th century is a theme that runs through this narrative. Denis Brenan Bullen, and probable fellow students of Woodroffe's school such as Denis Charles O'Connor, Henry Augustus Caesar, James Wherland, William Beamish and William Kearns Tanner, all shared these common student experiences where they became hardened to the sight and smells of human corpses in various stages of decay.

Unlike Dartnell, Bullen was not apprenticed to John Woodroffe. After training with his father, and possibly attending Woodroffe's course around the time of the Reade case, he went to Edinburgh in 1822 where he gained his Diploma from the Royal College of Surgeons and MD (Edin.). Having returned to Cork, he wrote in December 1825, aged 23, to the Lord Lieutenant asking to be appointed successor to William Hallaran as physician to the Cork Lunatic Asylum which Hallaran had founded. He claimed he was 'fully qualified' for the position which he believed to be in the gift of government.[17] In this he was mistaken and was told the Asylum was not in receipt of government funds or under the government's influence. In fact, the appointment was in the gift of the Governors of the Lunatic Asylum and the House of Industry and generated huge interest in the city. Candidates put their names forward publicly in the press, including John Woodroffe – who claimed as county surgeon he was legally entitled to the post.[18] Meetings were adjourned and reports were commissioned. Finally, on 28 February 1826, a meeting of 86 governors elected Dr Osborne as physician to the asylum at a salary of £100 and separately elected Edward Townsend as physician to the House of Industry at £50. A 'Moral Governor' was also appointed to oversee both medical officers at £150.[19] In all this Bullen played no part. Having gone directly to the Lord Lieutenant and been rebuffed, he withdrew from the fray. It is hard to believe that he didn't know in whose gift the appointment lay, but this was a time in Cork when power and privilege were in the grip of the Friendly Club, an exclusively Protestant 'political clique' that manipulated power to their own advantage.[20] Bullen may have been trying to circumvent the Friendly Club's influence (Osborne and Townsend were both members). Failure to secure Hallaran's post does not appear to have dented his self-confidence. Two years later, in 1828, he was chosen to lecture in Chemistry in the Royal Cork Institution where he would have mixed with Cork's scientific elite. No doubt, this helped him secure the job of junior surgeon in the North Infirmary in 1830. This was important because it gave him a clinical base in one of Cork's two charitable infirmaries and the prestige that went with it. He would soon put it to good use.

In 1830, Bullen was appointed secretary of the Munster Provincial College Committee with a brief to secure a Munster college for Cork. This was a slow burner and would trundle on for another decade before Queen's College Cork loomed into view. At a 'Great Provincial Meeting' in November 1838, with the Earl of Listowel in the chair, a petition was drafted to the newly enthroned Victoria, which began by recalling that 'Ireland already owes her only university to a Queen' and went on to hope that another Queen, 'who has already manifested the most favourable dispositions towards this country', would go on to found the next. A resolution was proposed by William Fagan, a wealthy butter merchant, and seconded by John Woodroffe, that 'the address which has now been read, be presented to the Queen'.[21] Denis Bullen put a lot of time and energy into this project, which he clearly saw as good for his native city and his own career.

He had hardly established himself in the North Infirmary when the Asiatic Cholera reached Cork in 1832, having emerged in Russia and Eastern Europe the previous year. As a response to the contagion, the two infirmaries agreed that all Cholera victims would be sent to the North Infirmary and that the South Infirmary would cater for all other cases until such time as the disease had spent itself. Fifteen years later Bullen would claim in his application for the Chair of Surgery in Queen's College that:

> In the year 1832 I took charge of nearly two thousand Cholera patients, which were received at the North Infirmary – at that time I published a work on Cholera, which was reprinted in most of the Journals of Great Britain and America.[22]

We do not know if Bullen was the instigator of this decision, the Municipal Corporation may have played a part and the medical profession in the city may have been consulted, but it is also true (and this made the South Infirmary's protestations of overwork gossamer thin) that the North Infirmary was at that time in a seriously dilapidated condition with no more than 28 beds and was probably not able for very much else.

The evidence for this comes from William Borrett MD who was an assistant commissioner in the Select Committee chaired by archbishop of Dublin, Richard Whately, to look into the state of the poorer classes in Ireland and was responsible for investigating the medical charities in Cork.[23] The North Infirmary was built in 1719 and initially comprised 24 beds. It was funded through the charitable donations of subscribers and later, a Grand Jury presentment. In the 18th century, subscribers were mostly the gentry and/or clerics who by subscribing a guinea a year, could recommend a poor person for intern treatment. When the patient recovered – or died – they could recommend another. The system was built on patronage that was meant 'to reinforce social difference and to induce gratitude towards wealthy benefactors on the part of the poor'.[24] Subscribers were not meant to recommend those who could pay for themselves, thereby eroding hospital income. This was one of many abuses. Another was that landowners in the wider county often refused to support the hospital even though their tenants would frequently appear at the gates requiring emergency admission. The abuse at the North Infirmary that most scandalized Borrett was one of negligent governance and its consequences – 'for the last forty years, there had been scarcely one regular meeting of the governors' and 'the remissness of the governing body has placed the entire control of the establishment in the hands of the apothecary'. The apothecary also happened to own a druggist's establishment in the city, from whence all medicines were procured at whatever price could be agreed between the apothecary and the druggist! Borrett concluded that:

> he has been in fact, not only the apothecary of the infirmary, but also the steward of the infirmary, the secretary of the infirmary, and, as far as could be learned, the board of the infirmary.[25]

Borrett drew a clear line between the medical gentlemen (among whom was Denis Bullen) and the Trustees, the Apothecary and the Treasurer: 'The correctness with which the duties of the physicians and surgeons have been discharged forms the only exception to the corrupt disorder which pervades every branch of the establishment'.[26] However, salvation was at hand and its instrument was Bullen's wife, Maria Ellen Power. Bullen described it thus:

> Prior to my appointment to the North Infirmary in the year 1829, Mr Anthony Sampayo, of Peterborough House Fulham, who had realized a very large fortune as a merchant connected with the city of Cork, being anxious to place at the disposal of the citizens of Cork a large sum of money for charitable purposes, and being a very intimate friend of the lady to whom I am married, placed in my hands the sum of 1,000*l.* to be applied to such charitable institution as I might wish to acquire a little influence in. The consequence of having this sum of money at my disposal was my election to the North Infirmary as surgeon.[27]

Antonio Teixeira Sampayo was from a wealthy Portuguese family. He married Frances Greatrakes (or Greatrix) of Cork in the early 1780s and had a large family by her. The Committee of Merchants supported him in a dispute with journeymen coopers in the 1790s and their minutes confirm that he had cellars in Cork.[28] He was a partner in Goold (or Gould) Brothers and Company, Irish importers of port wines. His brother, or cousin, Henrique Teixeira Sampayo, Conde de Povoa, was an immensely wealthy merchant who served as Portuguese Secretary of State for Financial Affairs between 1823 and 1825. He is credited in British parliamentary financial reports with almost single-handedly provisioning Wellington's army during the Peninsular War (1808–12). Between July and October 1811 he supplied 2,401,882 lbs of biscuit and transported large amounts of grain and flour from Egypt and the Americas throughout the campaign. He died in 1833 without being repaid. The matter was finally settled in 1840 by a payment of £113,025 4*s*. 11*d*. to his estate, or about one-third of what he had claimed.[29] Another Cork Sampayo, Theme Teixeira Sampayo, was the Portuguese Consul to Ireland and lived in Camden Place. Bullen moved into 4 Camden Place after his marriage to Maria Ellen Power so one possibility for the 'intimate friendship' is that the Power and Sampayo families were neighbours. Antonio Teixeira Sampayo, who provided the lead donation to the North Infirmary, was the signatory of over £17,780 of insurances for the South American commission. He had over $155,000 invested in the construction of Pennsylvania canals in 1831[30] and his principal residence was a London mansion, Peterborough House, Fulham. The Sampayo family were big timers and in this context their gift to Denis Bullen was not outrageously generous in terms of their overall wealth. It appears to have been calibrated to stimulate local effort, which in the end was not quite enough to realize the grand vision of a single General Infirmary for Cork. A John Power appears in the minutes of the Committee of Merchants in the 1790s and a Richard Power appears in another minute book dating from 1829. It is possible they were father and brother to Maria Ellen. They appear to have been butter exporters. Perhaps Sampayo provided the ships for their lucrative trade in salted butter to Lisbon and returned them to Cork laden with Portuguese sea salt and the Gould Brothers' finest port. The Sampayo family's wealth and the breath of their capitalist endeavours suggest many irons in different fires on both sides of the Atlantic. Mr Osborn Sampayo told a public meeting on 28 July 1829 that the family 'wished to place (funds) at the disposal of the Trustees of the North Charitable Infirmary, for the purpose of extending Hospital accommodation to the poor inhabitants of Cork'.[31]

A committee of six, including Bullen, was established then and there to raise further sums through a public appeal. A further donation of £350 from Anthony Sampayo came in November making a total donation of £1,050. To this was added a bequest of £500 from Thomas Rochford Esq. An identical bequest from Thomas Rochford also appears in the South Infirmary annual report of 1830 suggesting he left £500 to each infirmary, almost equalling the Sampayo gift. At the conclusion of the North Infirmary appeal the fund totalled £3,200 and discussions began on building a new 100 bedded hospital. At this point, some members of the County Infirmary in Mallow proposed amalgamating all three hospitals into one General Infirmary in which the County Infirmary would have a third of the beds and bear a third of the cost. The campaign for a General Infirmary in Cork continued for several years. While newspaper reports suggest most of the medical men in the city wanted it to happen, there were undercurrents of resistance. The governors of the North and South Infirmaries were less than enthusiastic and one even senses that Denis Bullen, who controlled the fund, was ambiguous. The proposed site on Lapp's Island was owned by Thomas Cuthbert Kearney, a trustee of the failed Cotter and Kellett's bank which ceased trading in 1809 and in 1832 still owed the public the sum of £691,000.[32] There may have been other reasons but the final outcome was the abandonment of the proposal. The South Infirmary refused to contribute any of their property or investments and the North Infirmary subscribers walked away from the table bringing the residue of the Sampayo funds with them. A site was found on the North Infirmary land at no cost and a new 110 bed hospital was built, which survived till 1987.

Bullen was philosophical about the outcome but he could see the bigger picture too and was bitter that the Cork infirmaries had such a low priority with local and national government. In his evidence to the Municipal Corporation enquiry, he testified that:

> except £100 for the two Infirmaries, there is not a single grant from Government for the support of the medical Institutions and Charities in this city. There was a grant, as I have stated, for a Lock-ward at the South Infirmary, but that has been withdrawn, and yet all the charities in Dublin receive large sums from the Government.[33]

What incensed him most was the £7,000 expended annually on Cork's Foundling Hospital. Bullen, as a good Catholic and struggling infirmary surgeon, thought that 'Foundling Hospitals, on a general principle, are the most pernicious to the morals, and repugnant to the general feelings of society; and in my opinion, the Hospital in this City is particularly objectionable'.[34] He was referring of course to Catholic society because the foundling hospitals took in children who were mostly born of Catholic mothers and brought them up as Protestants.

We cannot be sure what prompted Antonio Sampayo's gift. Undoubtedly there was more to it than simply assisting the career of a family friend. Sampayo lost his wife in 1815 and his daughter in 1830. He himself died in June 1832 after a long illness so possibly he saw his end coming and wanted to ensure his place in Heaven, much like the noble Gaelic families who endowed religious foundations in medieval Ireland.

Bullen provided his services to the North Infirmary *gratis*. The other two physicians and one surgeon were paid £20 per annum.[35] At the launch of the fundraising campaign for the new hospital, Denis and his brother William had each contributed £10 and their father £20. As individual donations these sums hold up well with others made at the launch so it seems correct to conclude that the family were comfortably off, generous, and committed to the public good. Indeed there is no evidence in any of the material on Denis Bullen that he was ever concerned about his own personal income. At the same time his public success in bringing in the Sampayo gift and doubling the amount through a fundraising campaign made his name in the city and extended the life of the North Infirmary by 150 years.

The young Bullen had his hands full and it is to his credit that he accepted the challenge and largely succeeded in turning the hospital around. Before Sampayo's serendipity, the North and South Infirmaries combined could only muster about 34 beds between them at an annual cost of £2,000. This does not include the Lock Ward in the South Infirmary reserved for syphilis cases. This was the subject of a separate government grant that was withdrawn about 1831 leading to its closure. On several different occasions Bullen gives different figures for hospital income and numbers of beds. In part this can be explained by the ebb and flow of hospital fortunes over time. Then as now, the only real way of saving money when times were lean was to close beds. The North Infirmary's 16 beds were 'necessarily reserved for the reception of casualties which require the immediate assistance of a surgeon, to the total exclusion of those numerous medical cases which equally demand the accommodation of an hospital.' Bullen was horrified by the mismanagement of the hospital:

> I could never have imagined till I was elected to the North Infirmary anything so monstrous, anything so extraordinary, as the manner in which I found the public funds administered in that and other medical institutions, proving the want of official inspection and control.[36]

Much later in his career he would report its trustees to the Poor Law Commissioners for misappropriating £300 and calling for an enquiry[37] which indirectly led to further reforms, including, six months after his death, the arrival of the French Sisters of Charity into the hospital to nurse on the Catholic wards.[38]

The impact he made in the North Infirmary brought him to the attention of the authorities as someone who could deliver Cork's medical gentlemen. When the Wyse Select Committee needed evidence on medical education in 1835, it was to Bullen they turned, and when the Hamilton Select Committee on Medical Charities in Ireland needed evidence on Cork's medical charities in 1843, it was to Bullen they turned too. Before any of this, when the Lord Lieutenant was charged with implementing the Anatomy Act in Ireland, following its passing into law in 1832, it was Denis Brenan Bullen he invited to be Inspector of Anatomy for the Province of Munster.

2. The Anatomy Act

The first Anatomy Bill was sponsored by Henry Warburton, MP for Bridport, in 1828. Warburton had been elected to Parliament for the Whig party two years previously and was already a respected scientist and a Fellow of the Royal Society. The Bill emerged out of the work of a Parliamentary Select Committee which he chaired. Its subject was medical education, especially English and Scottish medical education, and its focus was anatomy. Warburton took most of his evidence from medical teachers and practitioners but he also included, on promise of anonymity, two self-confessed professional 'resurrection men' who were known simply as A.B. and C.D. Having decided to propose a model similar to that used in France, where the unclaimed bodies of the poor were provided under a regulated system that included funeral rites and burial in consecrated ground, he tested this out on parish officers and vestrymen to see if it would work in Great Britain and Ireland.

The two witnesses called to give testimony on the French system were both Irish – James Richard Bennett (1797–1831) from Cork who demonstrated privately to English speaking students in Paris in the mid-1820s,[1] and David Barry (1780–1835), an army doctor from Roscommon, who received his entire medical training in the École Médicine, Paris and was a confirmed Francophile.[2] Their evidence was that about 200 English students travelled to Paris every year to gain an experience in dissection that they could not obtain in London. Both witnesses testified to the great superiority of the French system. Bennett, though, observed that dead bodies were less easily procured as formerly in Paris because of 'priests interfering, and prevailing on the friends of the persons to bury them'.[3] When these recent difficulties in Paris were put to the previous witness, James Somerville, MD (who would become the first Inspector of Anatomy for England), his reply was more forthright, and probably more prejudiced: 'The priests in France have always beheld with great jealousy the progress made by medical students; the priests are rather anxious to check the study of medicine, or to lower it'.[4] Tension between the Catholic church and the medical profession over possession of the dead was therefore not just an Irish phenomenon but arose universally from the Church's response to what it saw as a defilement of the human body that fell unfairly on the poor and caused uncomfortable questions for itself about resurrection and the afterlife. Protestant clergy shared their discomfort as we shall see from the testimony of the third Irish witness.

That witness was James Macartney (1770–1843), Professor of Anatomy at Trinity College Dublin.[5] What makes Macartney's evidence useful is the way he decides to review the whole subject in his opening remarks. He was a demonstrator to John Abernethy (1764–1831) in London in 1798 when 'bodies were abundant and could be procured for the price of from one to two guineas' and there were only three hospital schools and two private schools, 'altogether about 300 anatomical students'. He pointed out that 'the character of the resurrection men appeared to be very different from what is at present' which he attributed to 'the rarity of prosecutions' and the feeling among them that they were providing a service rather than committing a crime. However in the early decades of the 19th century, private schools increased rapidly in number. Resurrection men were employed by 'many different teachers' which led to 'contention' among them; demand outstripped supply:

> At the same time, the religious prejudices of the Scotch, respecting the sanctity of the dead body, seemed to come into operation in a very remarkable and unaccountable manner, so that every grave in the neighbourhood of Edinburgh and Glasgow began to be secured in such a way that it was made quite inaccessible.

In consequence, the resurrection men had to go further and further afield and this led to 'more frequent detections' and further precautions:

> These detections were published in the newspapers, and copied into the Irish papers; and to that may be attributed the origin or the prejudices or the excitement of the public feeling in Ireland upon the subject.[6]

Macartney's evidence suggests that the growth in demand for medical education on both sides of the Irish Sea, and the lack of regulation, gave rise to a situation where the procurement of bodies for dissection moved from an amateur sport among medical students and medical school porters to a quasi-professional occupation for resurrection men. These began to fall out among themselves as public hostility grew to the point where they were attacked and sometimes killed. Eventually the practice moved deep into the criminal underworld. Warburton's committee published its report in July 1828, before the exposure of the murderous activities of Burke and Hare in Edinburgh[7] and Bishop and Williams in London.[8] Nevertheless, even at this time Macartney says that 'within the last few months in the city of Dublin' a report originating in Scotland was being propagated 'that children were kidnapped for the purpose of dissection' and 'were to be sent over either to Scotland or England by steam vessels'.[9]

So by the time Warburton's committee sat, procurement of bodies for dissection had become an acute matter of public policy to the point where it eclipsed the deeper need for proper regulation of the medical schools. Even so, the Bill failed to pass through the House of Lords and it was only in 1832, after Burke, John Bishop and Thomas Williams had all been hanged and their cases had inflamed and terrified public opinion in equal measure that the final Bill, watered down, passed into law.

Unlike the French system, Warburton's Bill adopted an approach of light regulation and supervision. The French appointed a *Chef des Travaux Anatomiques* to implement the law. He had the assistance of three *prosecteurs* and three *aides d'anatomie*. Dissecting was centralized in two institutions in Paris, the Hôpital de la Pitié where private medical education took place, and the École de la Médicine which was a public institution. The inspectorate thus controlled the supply, carriage and dissection of bodies and ensured the proper religious rites and interment arrangements. Under the Anatomy Act of 1832, the Anatomy Inspectors had no such powers and no assistants to ensure the law was carried out properly. Bullen's main job as Inspector of Anatomy for the Province of Munster was to oversee the paperwork and make quarterly returns of the names, ages and causes of death of those whose bodies had been 'anatomized' in Cork. Violations of the Act were classified as misdemeanours rather than crimes. Punishment on conviction carried a maximum fine of £50 or three months in prison, at the discretion of the court. This would become a major stumbling block for Benjamin Alcock in 1852 but for most medical educators it was a clear signal that the spirit of the law was to enable the advancement of medical science, not to inhibit it.

The Anatomy Inspectorate was the first of twenty-three such inspectorates created between 1832 and 1875 so it was perhaps understandable that there were serious teething problems.[10] Ideas as to what it should actually do and what its powers should be differed according to what side of the debate one was on. The medical lobby wanted as little supervision as possible while the inspectors secured a reliable source of subjects. There were however those on the other side who saw the inspectors as protectors of the poor who should be empowered to prosecute on their behalf if wrongdoing was uncovered. Warburton was on the side of the medical lobby and saw the inspectorate as a 'precautionary measure' whose duties could be performed throughout Britain by just one man 'with the assistance of some policemen'.[11] Warburton won out and so from the very start the inspectors were compromised and under-resourced. Had they truly adopted the French approach things might have gone more smoothly, but centralization was associated with Napoleon and would have been unacceptable to any British parliament. As a result, an unhealthy secrecy surrounded their activities and against a background of limited powers, a growing politically aware working class, and a shortage in supply, they could only do their job by a combination of guile and persuasion. The inspectors' role was really to administer the system rather than to police it. They had no power to insist on bodies being handed over by those in legal possession of them – in most cases this meant the workhouse guardians – but if they were handed over, then the inspector required appropriate certification stating the name, age, sex, date, place and cause of death of the person, duly certified by a medical practitioner. This certificate had to accompany the body to the place of anatomical examination and the anatomist carrying out the examination had to provide that certificate to the inspector within 24 hours of the examination together with a certificate of interment in consecrated ground commensurate with the religious persuasion of the person. The anatomist had to copy the certificate into a book and produce it whenever required to do so by the Inspector.

A number of critical clauses were removed from the draft Bill during the committee stages. The first draft, omitted from the final Bill, provided that:

> it shall be lawful for every such Inspector to visit and inspect at any time, any Place where Anatomy is carried on, on the production by such Inspector of an Order written by direction of said Secretary of State, ordering such Inspector to visit and inspect such place.[12]

The consent clause was also watered down between the first and final Bill. In the first draft consent was stated positively by permitting anatomical examination 'with the Consent of the nearest known Relative of such Person' and a person could opt out during life by expressing this desire 'either in writing at any time, or orally in the presence of one or more witnesses'. In the final Bill, this was changed to:

> either in writing at any time during his life, or verbally in the presence of Two or more Witnesses during the illness whereof he died, that his Body after death might not undergo such examination, or unless the surviving Husband or Wife, or any known Relative of the deceased Person, shall require the Body to be interred without such examination.[13]

One might imagine, at the very least, that the Inspectors would have had power to authorize the places and practice of dissection in their jurisdictions but this was not so. Permission to dissect was conferred on any qualified medical practitioner provided:

> the Owner or Occupier of such place, or some party by this Act authorized to examine Bodies anatomically, shall, at least One Week before the first receipt or possession of a Body for such purposes at such place, have given Notice to the said Secretary of State, or Chief Secretary, as the case may be, of the Place where it is intended to practise Anatomy.[14]

This weakness in the legislation would cause Bullen, some twenty-six years later, to attempt to close down Henry Caesar's private school by asking the Royal College of Surgeons in London to withdraw recognition of his certificates.

The Anatomy Act was really a piece of social engineering to provide a regular supply of corpses to the medical schools to facilitate the proper training of doctors while causing the least offence to the political classes of the day. The source shifted from the plundered grave, which affected all classes, to the workhouse dead house, which affected the destitute only. The need for consent was worded in such a way as to make it almost impossible for those who in most cases could neither read nor write to withhold consent. Verbal consent could be withheld in the presence of two or more witnesses during the final illness but this was almost always in the workhouse infirmary where the power relationship between staff and paupers was heavily skewed in favour of the former. There was also the incentive that the cost of burial after dissection was a charge to the medical schools, which at least ensured burial in consecrated ground. By and large, this seems to have been honoured in Cork.

This then was the context in which, at the beginning of January 1833, Sir James Murray[15] was appointed Inspector for the Provinces of Leinster, Ulster and Connacht and Denis Brenan Bullen was appointed Inspector for Munster. The reason Murray, an Irish Catholic from County Londonderry, got the job was almost certainly because he had been appointed physician to the Lord Lieutenant in 1828, and continued in that role for over a decade as various Lords Lieutenant came and went. He was reliable and unflappable and appears to have enjoyed the great goodwill of the Dublin medical fraternity. In 1836 the Dublin anatomy teachers wrote to the Chief Secretary in glowing terms:

> The supply of bodies is amply sufficient for the purposes of instruction; the practice of exhumation (i.e., grave-robbing) is rendered unnecessary, and if perpetrated at all, is only resorted to by persons seeking for teeth for the use of dentists. For these most satisfactory consequences, we consider ourselves indebted principally to the judicious arrangements, official fairness, and praiseworthy impartiality of the Inspector, Sir James Murray.[16]

He kept in regular contact with the Chief Secretary in Dublin Castle to whom he sent on a quarterly basis the names, ages, cause of death and institutional address of all dead bodies sent to the medical schools. The vast majority came from the North and South Dublin Union workhouses. Murray never appears to have had any trouble sourcing subjects. This contrasted with London where there were constant difficulties.[17] As late as 1860, John South, the President of the Royal College of Surgeons of England, asked the Irish Chief Secretary for Murray's anatomical returns to 'lay them before government, and if possible induce them to render us such assistance in this important matter as is afforded to the Dublin schools'.[18] Thomas Larcom, the Under Secretary, and James Murray readily complied with South's request and sent him detailed returns for 300 bodies supplied to six schools from 1 January to 31 December 1860.[19] That there was comparative oversupply is not to say that there was not resistance from the public but over the years it diminished. Writing from Galway to the Chief Secretary in 1850, Murray was able to inform him that 'I rejoice to tell you that I find the clergy and people of my Church more willing to listen to reason than when I was last among them here'.[20] Murray, then, had some success in establishing the inspectorate in Dublin. He also had responsibility for Belfast and Galway but these cities were far less important than Dublin in terms of medical education. The other city with a thriving medical education scene at this time was, of course, Cork.

Bullen's role as Inspector for Munster was much lighter than Murray's. Effectively he was Inspector for Cork city and was never required to report on more than ten or twelve bodies in a quarter. He never used the pro-forma returns supplied by Dublin Castle, preferring to write a simple letter each quarter listing the names, ages and cause of death of the subjects dissected in Cork. He accepted his appointment in January 1833.[21] Cork's private medical schools were quick to apply to be recognized for the conduct of dissection. Only four days before, Christopher Bull had written asking to whom he should report the admission of unclaimed bodies at Woodroffe's school which had recently moved to Cove Street. Bull was a Trinity graduate and a colleague of Woodroffe's both as lecturer in his school and surgeon in the South Infirmary. Henry Caesar, proprietor of the Rutland Street school, was slower off the mark. He applied in November 1834 and received the Lord Lieutenant's warrant on 30 December. The newly appointed Inspector seems not to have permitted any dissections in the interim because Caesar wrote again on 20 December asking the favour of the Secretary of State 'of directing the Inspector to act by me as if a Licenced lecturer from the date of my former application'.[22] In April 1833, Bullen made his first quarterly returns, which he continued to do on the first day of the month following each quarter for the next 31 years. In his evidence to the Select Committee on Education in Ireland, Bullen stated in characteristically dogmatic tones that:

> I do not know any city which would present greater opportunities for an extensive school of medicine than Cork. There is a large pauper population, which enables us to cultivate the study of anatomy without having recourse to those unpleasant proceedings which other cities are obliged to do in order to procure a supply of bodies.[23]

This is a breathtaking statement from a man who, as student and as recently appointed Inspector, knew perfectly well that such unpleasant proceedings had taken place in Cork for two decades. Having given this evidence on 1 July he would go home and that same evening write a letter to the Chief Secretary, Lord Morpeth, certifying that Thomas Reardon, aged 50, cause of death, consumption, and Hannah Roche, aged 30, cause of death diarrhoea, had been dissected in the Cork schools of anatomy in the quarter just ended.[24]

When Bullen gave his evidence to the Wyse Committee he was correct in stating that Cork was well suited to an extensive school of medicine. As we have seen, it already had a number of private schools that ensured a regular supply of medical students to the universities of Glasgow and Edinburgh, and less commonly, Dublin. The earliest of these was Woodroffe's, established in 1811. Bullen, in his anatomical returns, also mentions a school of anatomy in Drinan Street. This appears to have belonged to Woodroffe's School of Physic and Surgery before he moved to Cove Street for the 1835/6 session. Reuben Harvey, one of his colleagues in the South Infirmary, continued to teach materia medica in Drinan Street for this session. The following year, Woodroffe and Bull moved again, this time to Warren's Place (now Parnell Place) where Woodroffe employed as his demonstrator a recent Cork graduate of Glasgow University, James Richard Wherland.[25] Woodroffe, unlike Wherland, appears never to have corresponded with Bullen as Inspector but to have relied on Reuben Harvey and Christopher Bull to do so on his behalf. Woodroffe probably treated the Anatomy Act with distain and regarded any correspondence with the Inspector with distaste. By 1838 he had ceased to teach independently from the South Infirmary and three years later, aged 60, he left Cork to return to his native Dublin.

A year after James Wherland had joined Woodroffe in Warren's Place, he set up the Cork School of Anatomy, Medicine and Surgery a few doors up the road. This was funded by his father, James Wherland senior, who spent £2,000 on it and 'at his own private expense, fitted up a Museum, Lecture room, Chemical apparatus &c.'[26] College Buildings, as it was generally known, was an elegant three-storey late Georgian building richly adorned with wrought iron work which he used as an engraving on his certificates. Wherland continued to lecture there until at least 1844. In December 1847 he applied unsuccessfully for the Chair of Anatomy and Physiology at Queen's College Cork. Later he became a guardian of the Cork Union and seems to have taken a great interest in the Cork Annuity Society, being secretary of it for many years. Another of his interests was hydropathy and the therapeutic use of hot water baths. His father also funded the Cork South district Lying-In hospital for the clinical benefit of his son. Like his mentor, John Woodroffe, James Wherland also gave public lectures:

> In 1844 and 1846, I delivered Popular Courses on Physiological Anatomy, as Knowledge essential to the Public, in preservation of Health and the prevention of disease. These were so well attended that the lecture room in the Cork Royal Institution could not contain the numbers that were anxious to attend.[27]

Henry Caesar returned to Cork with an MD from Edinburgh in 1828 and began to lecture in the Royal Cork Institution. In the 1830s he moved from his premises in Rutland Street to the South Mall and put considerable money into new dissecting facilities there. He had a distinctly edgy relationship with Bullen as Anatomy Inspector, which ended in full-blown enmity when Bullen tried to close him down in 1858. By 1845, Caesar's Cork School of Medicine was the only private school still running. He kept it going throughout the 1850s and even into the 1860s.

Bullen himself lectured to medical students, initially in the Cork Institution and later, after he was elected surgeon, in the North Infirmary. However, he never founded a medical school and never lectured in the schools founded by others. Denis Bullen celebrated his 35th birthday in June 1837. Up to that moment, his had been a stellar career of uninterrupted success. He had sailed through his medical education effortlessly and, by way of an advantageous marriage, had secured a financial windfall which he had used to re-invent Cork's ageing and ailing North Infirmary and obtain for himself a plum hospital surgeoncy in the process. He had adroitly manoeuvred his way between the Trustees of the North Infirmary and the South Infirmary's medical gentlemen (including his father's old enemy, John Woodroffe) by seeming to side publicly with both, but in the end he got his new 100 bed hospital on the north side of the city unfettered by any association with its rival on the south. With one bound he had moved to the head of Cork's medical elite and attracted government favour by being given responsibility for implementing the Anatomy Act in Cork. This was a national job of considerable prestige carrying a salary of £100 a year for not very much work, or so it seemed. He had also become the *de facto* spokesman for medical education in Cork and had been elected Secretary of the Provincial College Committee. These were Galilean days of joy when it seemed the name of Bullen could open all doors.

But there were two dark clouds on the horizon, both of which would in due course bring a deluge of misery on the city and change the nature of medical practice for all time. The first of these was the Poor Law (Ireland) Act and the second was the Great Famine. In the midst of both came the founding of Queen's College Cork bringing the promise of better times to come.

3. The best of times, the worst of times

Archbishop Whately's report on what to do about Irish poverty has been described as 'imaginative and constructive' but 'too radical for contemporary economic thinking'.[1] The government dropped Whately and turned instead to the English Poor Law Commissioner George Nicholls, who had no experience of Ireland. Nicholls was instructed to conduct a new inquiry that would recommend a system closely modelled on the English Poor Law. A Poor Law Act based on his recommendation of a national system of poor law unions each with a workhouse for indoor relief came into force in July 1838. The relief thus afforded 'was placed under the control of the English Poor Law Commission, and this body delegated Nicholls to exercise its functions in Ireland'.[2] Irish Poor Law Commissioners and Assistant Commissioners were appointed. Two of these, Doctors Denis Phelan and Maurice Corr, began to draw up a report on the medical charities of Ireland, as provided for by the Poor Relief Act which, besides its poor relief provisions:

> enjoined the Poor Law Commissioners to enquire into the existing medical charities, and to recommend any additional hospitals or dispensaries that might be required for the sick and convalescent poor in the different poor law unions.[3]

Denis Phelan was assisted by William James Voules, the local Assistant Poor Law Commissioner for Cork, in conducting the inquiry into the Cork Union. Voules attended the Cork Poor Law Guardians' meetings to keep them on the path laid out by the Poor Law Commissioners in Dublin. Armed with the evidence of Phelan, Corr and Voules, Nicholls recommended that the medical charities should be made part of the Irish poor law system and this was incorporated into the government's Medical Charities Bill presented to parliament in 1842 by Lord Eliot, the then Irish Chief Secretary. There followed what Laurence Geary calls 'a venomous summer of medical politics' led principally by members of the Royal College of Surgeons speaking through the *Dublin Medical Press*. Opinion in the provincial centres and among the hard-pressed dispensary doctors was more balanced, with many seeing the security of funding promised by the Poor Law as the lesser of two evils when set alongside control by government-appointed Commissioners. The source of that concern was not merely their distaste for having to maintain their subscriber lists every year, nor for having to require patients to produce a subscriber's ticket (and turn away those who did not) but because of an unexpected if predictable consequence of the Poor Law itself – a drastic collapse in private subscriptions and Grand Jury presentments for the infirmaries and dispensaries across the country caused by visceral objections to what the ratepayers saw as double taxation from the Poor Law and the Grand Jury cess. Bullen presented his own figures for the North Infirmary to the Hamilton Select Committee in 1844.[4]

Table 1

	Income 1839	Income 1840	Income 1841
North Infirmary	£1,369	£1,139 14s. 11d.	£834 7s. 8d.

The North Infirmary situation was more complex than at first met the eye, for the fall off in voluntary subscriptions during this period, revealed by further questioning, was £73 1s. 2d. whereas the Grand Jury presentment fell by £350 because the city's finances had also been hit by the new tax. A further loss of £85 15s. 6d. was caused by 'arrears not paid in on account of the death of the treasurer' – apparently the North Infirmary's governance problems identified by Borrett in 1835 had not been entirely sorted out.[5] Such losses were unsustainable and, apart from the arrears caused by the treasurer's untimely passing, were directly caused by the introduction of the Poor Law in Cork city and county.

Bullen also testified to the impact on Cork's business community who played a crucial role in supporting the medical charities. He based this on conversations with two prominent businessmen, John Gould, probable business partner of Anthony Sampayo, and James Daly. Both were members of the grand jury who 'took an active part in the fiscal concerns of the city'.[6] Bullen's primary interest seems to have been to secure stable long-term funding for the North Infirmary and to reform a system of medical relief that saw large numbers of rural tenants streaming into Cork city for sick relief with no obligation placed on their landlords to support them. He also wanted an end to the practice of extern patients appearing at multiple dispensaries and infirmaries with the same complaint. Apparently they did this in great numbers on the simple, if dangerous, principle that double the dose did you twice the good!

He could also see the damage caused by the so-called workhouse test of destitution; he believed work for the able-bodied was the answer, and that institutional relief should focus on the sick poor – 'remove the sick father or the sick child and relieve them, but do not incarcerate the able-bodied and those that are willing to work, in bastilles which are hateful to the people'.[7]

This was the substance of his arguments to the Select Committee. He was less measured in a letter to the *Southern Reporter* where he described the poor law 'spreading its desolating effects by uprooting property and fearfully adding to pauperism'.[8] The Select Committee challenged him on these remarks and on others he had made at a private medical meeting some months earlier where he talked about 'evil consequences' from 'the vindictiveness of the Commissioners' and their treatment of the medical profession:

> they will grind it to dust; they will care little for the services of the medical practitioner, or what duties they may have to perform, provided they can procure it at a cheap rate.[9]

He justified these remarks by distinguishing between those made at 'a private meeting of his medical colleagues' and his evidence to the Select Committee 'as a person charged by my fellow citizens with a public trust to consider their interests, and not the mere personal views and wishes that I may have as a medical man'. What is interesting about Denis Bullen is that, with one critical exception which we will come to later, he never denied what he had said. Rather he used the context to justify it. Later in his evidence, he talked about the freemasonry of professions:

> We all know there is a freemasonry in professions, which ought to be held sacred, and that he who violates that freemasonry, in so doing reflects very little honour either upon himself individually, or upon the profession to which he belongs ... but it is a very different thing when we stand before the tribunal of the public, as I stand now when we have to deal with great national interests.[10]

The Poor Law brought another change to Bullen's role as Anatomy Inspector; he found himself having to deal with an elected board of guardians answerable to the Poor Law Commissioners in Dublin with local Assistant Commissioner Voules frequently present at its meetings. This was a far cry from the lax governance of the house of industry and his own North Infirmary. In the early years of the Poor Law, the new guardians were anxious to do better than their predecessors, which led to tensions between those who wanted to ensure that 'expenditure was controlled and kept to the lowest possible level' and the more progressive ones who 'were determined to provide a better workhouse diet and easier access to outdoor relief'.[11] In practice, much depended on the competence of the Master and Matron. There were five masters during Denis O'Connor's seventeen years in the Workhouse Infirmary – 'the first master was an accountant, the second an unsuccessful apothecary, the third an insolvent tobacconist, the fourth a clerk of stores – but a man of great ability, the fifth a very respectable hotel-keeper'.[12]

Denis Charles O'Connor (1808–88) entered Trinity College Dublin on 24 May 1826 and graduated BA in 1831 and MB in 1834 having taken the Licentiate of the RCSI in 1833.[13] In his application for the Chair of Medicine at QCC in 1848 he claims to have obtained the highest honours in Science in his undergraduate course.[14] He would go on to be elected President of the British

Medical Association in 1879 during the meeting of the association in Cork and conferred with an honorary LLD by Cambridge University a year later.[15] He spent several years in Paris before returning to Cork in 1838, where he lectured in the practice of medicine at James Wherland's school in Warren's Place until it closed in 1844.[16] At this time he had already been Workhouse Medical Officer for four years.[17] His medical colleague was John Popham, BA, MD who was in charge of the workhouse fever hospital. The two laboured together all through the years of the Great Famine and the migration ships and both appear to have come through it with their humanity intact. While he accepted the legitimacy of the workhouse system his testimony was convincing on the hopeless inadequacy of the Cork Workhouse to cope with the destitute 'during those dreadful years from 1845 to 1855'. He fought a running battle with the guardians for better food for the paupers and 'a superior class of diet for the aged and infirm, without being registered as sick'.[18] The humanity he displayed throughout these years earned him the sobriquet of 'the angel doctor' among the citizens of Cork and the workhouse minute books bear testimony to his enlightened concern. He took an active part in the County and City of Cork Medical and Surgical Society in the 1850s and 1860s, one of the few Queen's College professors to do so.[19] 'His contributions to the medical literature were not numerous, but include papers published in the *Lancet* and in the *Dublin Quarterly Journal of Medical Science*'.[20] At the same time he understood and facilitated the passage of the unclaimed bodies of the poor to the medical schools and as we shall see in the next chapter, he was willing to recommend that the QCC Professor of Anatomy and Physiology might falsely claim to be a friend or relative of the deceased in order that a body might be secured and the letter of the Anatomy Act fulfilled.

His colleague John Popham entered Trinity College on 31 May 1825 aged 18. He was made Scholar in 1830, graduated BA in 1833 and MB in 1835. His years in Trinity exactly corresponded to O'Connor's. He taught Midwifery and the diseases of Women and Children in Wherland's school from 1838 to 1844 but unlike O'Connor, failed to obtain a post in the new College. The two attended Mr Sullivan's school in Cork and probably received their first training in anatomy at John Woodroffe's school. If they were not already friends when they entered the Workhouse, they could not have survived the nightmare of the Cork Workhouse for so many years unless there had been a strong bond of understanding between them.

The Cork House of Industry building was situated just to the north of, and adjacent to, the South Infirmary on Langford Row. Hallaran's lunatic asylum comprised the third building in a complex site on the higher ground to the south-east of Douglas Street and the South Terrace.[21] It had been used as the workhouse in the early years of the Poor Law. Built in 1743, it was viewed with suspicion and dread by the poor.

There were many in Cork, Bullen included, who believed that the house could be renovated and extended and that a proposed new building further out from the city on the Douglas Road was a needless expense. A group of medical gentlemen, and a few reverend gentlemen sent a memorial to the Lord Lieutenant seeking an examination into the 'insalubrity' of the proposed site which they claimed was marshy and unhealthy. Phelan and Voules conducted a spiky examination of Woodroffe, Caesar, Townsend, Tanner, Lloyd, O'Connor, Sir James Pitcairn and others over four days in which the arguments of the memorialists were gradually undermined and eventually demolished by the evidence of Denis Bullen, Denis O'Connor and Sir James Pitcairn.[22] For example, it emerged that Caesar owned a nearby site he wished to sell while Woodroffe lived nearby and was probably concerned about the value of his property. Bullen broke ranks with his medical brethren and said that the proposed site was no better and no worse than any other. O'Connor gave his evidence on the third day and effectively won it for Phelan. He 'entirely dissented' from the memorial, basing his opinion on 'private and public practice in the neighbourhood of the site for three years as Dispensary Physician' from 1834 to 1837 'but my private practice in attending the poor gratuitously there has continued'. Four years later, Bullen stated to the Hamilton Commission that he considered the new Workhouse 'as lavish and useless as any expenditure could possibly be; an expenditure of 25,000*l*'.[23] What he may have failed to realize was that the charitable infirmaries were being slowly replaced by a massive public infirmary in the workhouse complex. The opportunity for a large general charitable infirmary in 1835 had been lost for ever.

The new guardians were proud of 'being the first union declared in Ireland'.[24] Their first meeting took place in the House of Industry on 4 June 1839 and almost the first topic considered was whether or not to admit gentlemen of the press to their meetings, 'without which they would not have that Confidence which publicity produces'. The Poor Law Commissioners refused on the grounds that it would 'invite display in debate and prove obstructive of the deliberate and expeditious dispatch of business'.[25] It was an early example of English practice being imported to Ireland without regard to local culture and it didn't work. Anonymous leaking to the press was as common then as now. Nine months later a report appeared in the *Southern Reporter* that required an immediate and robust response from the Inspector of Anatomy.

The Matron, Catherine Horgan, had reported that a number of girls and women had escaped through a sewer into the yard of the South Infirmary next door and on being called back had been followed through the sewer by two medical apprentices 'cursing and swearing in a most vehement manner'. This report prompted Joseph Hayes, one of the guardians, to describe an even greater outrage that had taken place 'within a week or two of the time when the house had been surrendered to the Board'. A pauper died in the House and his body not being claimed, was given to the South Infirmary for dissection. Dissection followed, and:

when those Students had indulged in all the barbarities that imagination can connect with their practices, they sallied forth from their dissecting den, and with parts of the unfortunate deceased in their bloody and disfigured hands, ran through the female wards, thrusting them in the faces of the inmates, and smearing them with human gore. They carried the heart of the deceased in a tin vessel, exposing it to the frightened gaze of the poor people, who were unable to fly or avoid the savage exhibition.

This lurid account prompted scandalized calls for a prosecution from at least one guardian until the voice of Voules – an experienced bureaucrat who knew exactly what the law could and could not do – was heard over the clamour:

> I do not profess to be the legal adviser of the Board in any proceedings outside the Poor Relief Act – but I still think the best plan will be for me to summon the parties before this Board, on next Monday, when two Justices of the Peace will be present – for there are over thirteen on the Board – and then the Chairman can read the youths a lecture which they or the public will not readily forget.[26]

The next issue of the paper published Bullen's response to Hayes:

> there has been no licenced School of Anatomy in either the House of Industry or in the South Infirmary. If, therefore, the practice of Anatomy has been carried on by any parties whatsoever in these Establishments, it has been a gross violation of the Anatomy Act, and the parties so offending have made themselves liable to very heavy penalties.[27]

He went on to request specific information that might lead to 'a summary conviction'. It was bluff and bluster as no licence was required, only notice of intent. Hayes probably knew this as he undertook to substantiate his charge with the 'particulars of the evidence by which I can uphold it'. There is no evidence that Bullen took the matter further. The guardians, on the other hand, did follow through with Voules' advice, their minutes of 6 April resolved that the culprits 'having attended the Board and offered a sufficient apology that they be now called in and admonished, which done accordingly'.[28]

The next matter that required the Inspector's attention occurred at the turnpike of the Western Road on Monday 6 February 1843. When the turnpike man asked what was in a box being carried by a horse and cart (so as to determine the correct toll), the carter claimed ignorance. On opening the box, the body of a 46-year-old man was discovered, together with a note from Dr Richard Madras of Coachford Dispensary to Dr James Wherland of College Buildings, Warren's Place, stating that the corpse was being sent in accordance with the provisions of the Anatomy Act (1832). However, there were a number of suspicious circumstances: all the teeth had been extracted and the body had been doubled up and placed in a box not more than three feet long and eighteen inches wide. It was conveyed to the Bridewell, together with the carter, his wife and a boy, while further enquiries were made. Dr Bullen advised an inquest at which it emerged that the body was that of Patrick Lane who had died and been buried in Aghabullogue Cemetery. The carter and another man were found guilty by a jury of stealing the body and grave clothes but with a recommendation for leniency. The two doctors were not prosecuted but both were the subject of opprobrium 'both loud and deep' from the crowd outside the court.[29] Bullen could have insisted on prosecution but chose not to, probably having consulted higher authority. The judge described the two doctors as 'the prime movers in the transaction' but then added:

> We believe we may say that the Government will not proceed against them for penalties, on the ground that certain public bodies in Cork have set themselves up in opposition to the law, and have deprived them of the means the law allows them, of procuring a knowledge of their profession, which is much desired for the well-being of society.[30]

These remarks illuminate how the judiciary viewed the Anatomy Act. The honourable judge was probably referring to the Workhouse guardians who, some months after the student rampage, had passed another resolution that 'the Board of Guardians cannot sanction the giving up for anatomical purposes the Bodies of such Persons as shall occasionally die in this Establishment'. They were not compelled to do so but by refusing, the private medical schools reverted to their old ways. The carters were prosecuted for stealing the body and grave-clothes, a crime that carried a penalty of transportation but because of the jury's recommendation, they only got twelve months imprisonment.[31] At this time, both Workhouse doctors – O'Connor and Popham – were lecturing in Wherland's school. Did they know what was going on? Almost certainly they did. It may have been at this time, long before Queen's College opened its gates, that the solution of pretending to be relatives of unclaimed deceased paupers was first thought of.

Friday 9 May 1845 was a red letter day for Cork and for Denis Brenan Bullen. Thomas Wyse, MP for Waterford, had first raised the need for provincial colleges in Ireland in a speech to the House of Commons in July 1831.[32] He had chaired the Select Committee on Education in Ireland in 1835 to which Bullen had testified. Bullen had been one of the leaders on the Provincial Colleges Committee since its inception. Wyse had repeatedly tried to get the government to take notice of the pressing need for a more broadly based system of higher education that would follow on from the successful non-denominational national education system introduced in 1831. On this memorable Friday, Sir James Graham, the Secretary of the Home Department in Peel's Conservative government, rose to his feet to seek leave of the House to bring forward a Bill for the establishment of three academic institutions in Ireland, one in the north, one in the south and one in the west. Of Cork, he said:

> Seeing that it has an immense population, and that there is an important medical school established there at this moment, seeing that it is easy of access – also that it has a very large population surrounding it – for these, and many other reasons, and especially on the ground of the strong feeling which I find to coexist in that locality in favour of some such institution, I should say Cork would naturally be the site of one of the Colleges for the south of Ireland.[33]

He was proposing to provide £100,000 capital and £18,000 annual endowment to cover all expenses. This was divided equally among the three Colleges – £33,000 capital and £6,000 recurrent for each. Theology and religion would not be on the syllabus but private individuals could endow these subjects. The government reserved the right to appoint and dismiss the professors if good cause was shown. It was warmly welcomed by speaker after speaker. Only two, the Member for the University of Oxford and the Member for Dungarvan spoke against, the former, a rather small-minded Protestant, presciently describing it as 'a gigantic scheme of Godless education'. The Provincial Colleges Committee met in Cork on 20 May to decide their response. Bullen began by giving 'his approbation to the spirit of liberality and generosity which had characterized the introduction of the Bill into Parliament'. He proposed they should express their 'strongest approbation of the measure as far as it went'. Others were less generous, or perhaps more suspicious, and the final resolution – also proposed by Bullen – totally failed to match the grandeur of the Parliamentary debate:

> That we approve of the spirit in which the question of Academical Education has been brought before Parliament, and consider the grant to be provided liberal, and calculated to effect the objects for which this Committee has been constituted.[34]

Mr Craig thought the resolution 'milk and water' but it passed unanimously nonetheless. Graham thus set in train a series of events: the Bill was passed; Queen's Colleges were established in Belfast, Galway and Cork; Sir Robert Kane was appointed President in Cork and chairs were advertised in all three Colleges. In academic terms this was a seismic event. Applications poured into Dublin Castle, elaborate memorials were printed, references from distinguished past pupils were sought. A new academic elite, heretofore confined to Trinity College and the College of Surgeons, was literally created by a stroke of the royal pen.[35]

There were four medical chairs and a total of 86 applicants: Anatomy and Physiology (31); The Practice of Medicine (21); Materia Medica (21); Surgery (13).

All were anxious to present themselves and their achievements in the best possible light. Bullen himself applied for the chair in surgery. The most interesting aspect of his application is how he described his contribution to obtaining a provincial college for his native city. After being 'unanimously elected Professor of Chymestry in the Royal Cork Institution' in 1828 he 'laid before the Proprietors a detailed prospectus for establishing the Munster Provincial College' (which he included in his application). 'This was the commencement of the proceedings, that ultimately led to obtaining the Colleges Act'. Unfortunately this does not seem to have survived so we cannot be certain whether he was gilding the lily or was factually correct in claiming authorship of the first document to propose a provincial college for Cork. His one referee was William Roche, brother of James. There is a sense that the surgery chair was his for the asking and that his application was a formality.

This was not the case with Henry Caesar, who applied for the Anatomy and Physiology chair. Caesar provided a whole series of documents with his application, including 27 testimonials from his former pupils and a group testimonial from 20 licenced apothecaries and medical practitioners in Cork. He even included testimonials from Catholic pupils and clergy stating that they had never heard him making any 'allusion that could be hurtful to our feelings or principles as Roman Catholics'. Finally he added a resolution from the Directors of the Cork Mechanics Institute thanking him for 'the highly instructive Course of Lectures on Human Physiology, which he delivered gratuitously to a very large class of Members of this Institute'. There was something desperate about Caesar's application. No stone was left unturned. He gave the game away when he wrote 'that the endowed College in Cork, must so far surpass any private establishment, as to ruin memorialist's present school, and if so his large family unless your Excellency be pleased to appoint him to the Chair of Anatomy'.[36] His prediction came true, he having failed both on this occasion and five years later to secure the chair he longed for. The other medical school proprietor was James Wherland who applied for the Anatomy chair in competition with Caesar. His application was a simple statement of his qualifications and experience as lecturer and proprietor of his school.[37]

Some of the lecturers at these schools such as Thomas Gregg and William Beamish also applied. Beamish was physician to Cork's County and City Jails and the 'son of the oldest member of the Medical Profession in the city'.[38] Beamish went for the political elite for his referees – Lord Viscount Bernard MP, Daniel Callaghan MP, William Fagan MP, Mr Sergeant Murphy and Major Beamish, High Sheriff elect of Cork City. One of his pupils who vouched for him was Nathaniel Hobart who would play a crucial role in the controversy that came to surround the successful applicant – Benjamin Alcock – and would himself apply for Alcock's vacant chair in 1854.

Denis O'Connor applied for the chair for the Practice of Medicine. His application was very formal, each paragraph beginning 'That Memorialist ... is

Physician to the Cork Union Workhouse', or 'has been at all times anxious for the acquisition of knowledge and for its diffusion among his fellow citizens'. He submitted 'these facts with the accompanying testimonials for your Excellency's consideration'.[39] O'Connor was certainly not guilty of exaggeration and it is likely that his reputation for integrity and dedication did more to ensure his appointment than anything in his memorial.

Famine began in earnest in the winter of 1847. When the numbers of dead were rising by the week, it became in the guardians' interest to pass the cost of their disposal to the medical schools. At this stage, the building of the Queen's College was underway and Caesar's school was the only private medical school left in the city. The citizens of Cork were seeing steadily rising numbers of destitute and starving people in their streets and any outrage they may have felt at the dissection of human bodies by anatomists and students quickly dissipated. A newspaper report in 1866 quoted the High Sheriff as saying 'the custom of giving dead bodies for the purposes of science had existed for the previous nineteen years'.[40] This remark was made in the context of another workhouse body scandal and suggests a temporary change in custom and practice brought about by the Famine rather than a policy change of heart by the guardians.

Surviving correspondence involving Denis Bullen reveals little of the impact of the Famine on his life and work. We have seen already that his mother was known for her piety and good works. In 1837 she started an infant school 'to counteract the effect of a similar institution which had been established by Protestants in the parish'.[41] During the Famine years, she provided food for the children to take home to their families.[42] Denis almost certainly involved himself in the medical care of these children and their families. His father had died in 1844 and by that stage Bullen himself had a young family. We also know from his evidence to parliamentary commissions that both infirmaries were already turning away extern patients and can only guess how much more stressful it must have been to turn away those who were starving as well. He attended meetings of the medical profession that continued during the Famine years. Running costs of the charitable institutions and control by 'respectable and responsible members of the medical profession' continued as major preoccupations.[43] By 1849, they were calling for a full blown 'Medical Department' in Dublin Castle:

> to which shall be entrusted everything connected with the various Medical Institutions, the Lunatic Asylum, the registration of vaccination, births and deaths, as well as the various sanitary arrangements which are now becoming increasingly important.[44]

Throughout the Famine he continued sending his quarterly reports to Dublin. He wrote on 1 January 1851 that he had not 'received the usual certificates of interment from Dr Caesar for the subjects which had been received into his school since October 10th 1849' and begged to enclose Caesar's reply to his request for an explanation which was that 'there is no regular sexton to St John's burial ground' to complete the paperwork. Caesar promised to send the certificate when he found the acting sexton who must have recorded the interments and under normal circumstances would have certified the names at the end of the teaching year. This seems to have been Caesar's normal practice. Bullen did not normally forward any certificates of interment to Dublin Castle, so exactly why he saw fit to challenge Caesar at this time and forward his reply to the Castle is not obvious. It does however tell us where Caesar buried his dissected bodies during these years.

The Famine affected the lives of everyone in Cork as more gaunt and starving people sought refuge in the city. Denis O'Connor and John Popham were at the front line and experienced at first hand the tide of human misery that flowed into the Workhouse Infirmary. They kept pleading with the guardians for more space. At the end of October 1846, they drew attention to 'the crowded state of the Workhouse' containing 3,200 in a building intended for 2,000 'with a probable increase according to the rate of admissions during the last few weeks, of 200 a week.' O'Connor was not a man to dramatize, but in the same report, he added 'the resources of the building are completely exhausted. We feel sure that the House cannot without danger receive any further increase of Inmates'.[45] They further warned of 'dangerous attacks of pulmonary disease' during the forthcoming winter, particularly on 'aged persons and children'. Nobody realized the scale of what they were facing into that winter. The Poor Law Commissioners in Dublin wrote on 21 November saying that 'the number sanctioned by the joint authority of the Medical Officers should be on no account exceeded' otherwise the guardians would become responsible for 'any evil consequences which may issue in regard to the sanitary conditions of the Workhouse'. If this meant rejecting paupers at the gate, then 'the facts should be stated in their minutes and the names and residencies of the persons so refused communicated without delay to the Relief Committee of the District within which the parties reside'.[46] O'Connor however would not refuse a dying patient no matter what the Commissioners in Dublin might say. The Cork guardians reported 132 deaths at their weekly meeting on 19 April 1847, adding:

> It is proper to observe that most of those admitted during the week were persons who were dying at the gate and were taken in by the directions of the Physician of the establishment, Dr O'Connor.[47]

The guardians set in train a building programme for temporary accommodation. The doctors again being asked for their opinion stated that 4,350 was 'the utmost number which these buildings may be allowed to contain with any security for health.' By January 1850, the Master was reporting to the board that 'the inmates in the Penitentiary and the Hospital Wards are also overcrowded, there being now in some of the hospital wards four in a bed and in the Children's Ward six, seven and eight in a bed'.[48]

O'Connor and Popham were not the only medical officers in Cork to feel the full effects of famine. William Beamish, medical officer of the county and city jails, who would succeed Bullen as Inspector of Anatomy, and who had applied unsuccessfully for one of the QCC medical chairs, wrote to the Chief Secretary looking for a rise in pay on 31 October 1850. From his home in Camden Place (by this time he and Bullen were neighbours), he wrote:

> previous to the year 1847 the average daily number of Prisoners (in the County Jail) did not exceed 250 and the daily average number in Hospital 7. Whereas since then the daily average number has been 1,200 including 200 convicts, and the hospital 90 ... the (City) Jail this day contains one hundred and eleven male convicts.[49]

This was so far beyond what he could have anticipated when he was appointed that he requested a rise from his salary of £74 per annum for both jails. His plea fell on deaf ears. A note in red on the letter reads 'Inform that His Excellency has no power to order any remuneration to be paid to Officers of County Gaols for their attendance on Convicts who may be detained therein'.[50]

4. Alcock

Benjamin Alcock is best known today for his discovery of Alcock's canal, an anatomical structure in the pelvis, also called the pudendal canal, through which the internal pudendal artery, internal pudendal veins, and the pudendal nerve pass. The eponym places him at the forefront of anatomists of his day. However, it is when we examine his brief but controversial tenure of the Chair of Anatomy and Physiology at Queen's College Cork that the full picture of the outworking of the Anatomy Act in Cork comes into focus. Alcock was not the first choice for the chair. According to O'Rahilly, he was appointed in place of Alexander Carte, 'who has been obliged to retire because of ill-health'.[1] Carte's withdrawal left the way open to the new President, Sir Robert Kane, to suggest Alcock for the role.

Kane and Alcock had worked together in Apothecaries' Hall in Dublin's Cecilia Street in the early 1830s and Kane had a high regard for Alcock.[2] Later, when the QCC row blew up, Kane wrote a long letter to the Chief Secretary admitting that 'I took the liberty of recommending his appointment to Lord Clarendon, then Lord Lieutenant ... had I not done so, Dr Alcock would not have been appointed'.[3] Kane knew about Alcock's quarrelsome history and took an enormous gamble in appointing him. When it failed, Alcock lost his chair and his profession and also, very probably, a higher place in the pantheon of 19th-century Irish anatomists.

Benjamin Alcock was the son of Nathaniel Alcock (1770–1836), medical officer of the Kilkenny dispensary, who married Deborah Prim, daughter of John Prim Esq. of Ennisnag, Co. Kilkenny in 1798. Baptized on 19 May 1801, Benjamin was the eldest of three sons and at least two daughters.[4] The dispensary was established in 1814 for people in the liberties of Kilkenny and investigated by William Borrett of the Whately Commission in 1835 (Borrett interviewed Alcock) and by Denis Phelan of the Nicholls Commission in 1841 (by which time Alcock had been dead for five years). Neither was complimentary and together they support his granddaughter's assessment that his professional life had been a hard one, and had aged him prematurely. Both were also highly critical of the total lack of oversight from the governors of the Charity. Alcock earned £50 Irish per year and did not admit to having any sizeable private practice, but claimed he could not attended any other dispensary because 'the duties of the one under my care are so overwhelming, the district extending about 40 square miles, and thickly inhabited by very poor people'.[5] Better-off citizens of Kilkenny paid their own private practitioners rather than use the dispensary and subscribers deserted it in numbers. No records had been kept and returns appeared fictitious to Denis Phelan and his colleagues.[6] His granddaughter Deborah, on the other hand, quotes family tradition that:

> Dr Alcock was a fine specimen of the old-world physician and gentleman, trusted and loved by rich and poor, and commending himself to all by strict integrity and active benevolence. In his own household he ruled with a firm though kindly hand; and was regarded with that wholesome and beautiful 'filial fear' which, far from lessening affection, broadens and deepens its current.[7]

All the boys went to Kilkenny College as day pupils and then to Trinity College where they performed well, Benjamin taking first place in the entrance examination. It seems that money was short but aspirations were high. This may have put unreasonable pressure on the boys to perform, particularly the eldest.

Trouble began at Apothecaries' Hall where Alcock held the Chair of Anatomy.[8] In September 1838, the premises at Cecilia Street were nearing completion and the cost was borne by the professors according to the following scheme:

Table 2

Chair	Proportion of capital cost
Anatomy	£230
Materia Medica	£145
Chemistry	£230
Surgery	£145
Practice of Medicine	£145
Midwifery	£145
Botany	£125
Forensic Medicine	£125
Total	£1,290

The eight professors also had to pay rent, taxes, repairs, insurance, painting, legal expenses, common advertising and the salary of one porter. Anatomy and Chemistry had each to pay a quarter of the coal bill and the rest paid the remaining half in equal proportions. Dissection room and laboratory costs added to the Anatomy and Chemistry costs so Alcock and the Professor of Chemistry bore the most. Both of these professors held their special premises in trust for the School.[9] For the 37-year-old Alcock, this was a major investment that he would have to recoup from student fees.

The first quarrel was sparked in 1846 when the Professor of Surgery, Andrew Ellis, raised his surgery fee for students who attended Alcock's class. Alcock took offence because this penalized his students and potentially led them to consider other schools. He claimed that Ellis had circulated a story that somebody, presumably another professor, had 'sworn that I had requested him to send his pupils to attend surgery at some other school than that of Cecilia-street, or interfered directly with students to prevent them from joining Mr Ellis's class'. Alcock hotly denied 'this calumny'. There were two bouts of public correspondence between the two before the row subsided. Alcock seems to have had the last word in print when he wrote to *Saunders Newsletter* on 11 November 1846 to suggest that Ellis, when he realized Alcock was going public, quietly dropped his differential fee for Alcock's students. Instead of also quietly dropping the matter, as might have been politic, Alcock went ahead with a full-blooded public attack on Ellis. In this last letter, he felt 'under the painful necessity' to rub Ellis's nose in the fact that he had been forced to accept Alcock's students 'without any distinction in his fee between them and the Pupils of other Lecturers <u>before</u> he had been forced publically to admit the fact in the newspapers'.[10] Alcock's sensitivity to insult combined with a meticulous intelligence must have made him difficult to deal with in any kind of collegial setting. The outcome of this particular spat was a resolution passed by the professors that none of them should in future publish any document bearing on the interests of the School or its professors without submitting it to the majority of the professors.[11] It was a truce at best.

The second quarrel came when Alcock was offered the QCC chair and therefore had to resign from the Hall. This brought into play clause six of the agreement between the governors of the Hall and their professors which allowed a retiring professor to recoup his investment from his successor.[12]

By submitting his resignation, Alcock was taking on trust that he would get his money back. The value he placed on his interest was £500. He claimed that the secretary, Robert D. Speedy, 'induced' him to resign with an assurance that 'no one should be returned who did not satisfy me in the price which I put on the Chair'.[13] Henry Corbett, who was the only candidate, offered £400.[14] The other professors declined to make up the difference 'in consequence of the depressed state of the Medical Schools of Dublin as well as of the establishment of Rival Schools in the Provinces'.[15] Alcock managed to get his hands on the Deed of Partnership and refused to surrender it 'unless he received a guarantee that he should have the use of it when he required it'.[16] He then put the whole matter in the hands of his solicitor, Mr Baillie, who returned the Deed on receipt of the guarantee. The Court of Directors of the Hall were called upon and an arbitration process was agreed. Alcock appointed Dr Robert Smith[17] and the professors appointed Dr Philip Bevan. The arbitrators met the parties separately on 1 and 2 November and ruled that the chair 'together with the property thereto belonging' were worth 'Four Hundred pounds sterling and <u>no</u>

more'.[18] Alcock had to accept this but probably took up his new post in Cork with a residual sense of grievance. It seems to have been the last time he trusted anyone.

Kane knew of both quarrels.[19] He actually held the Chair of Chemistry at the Hall when the first row with Ellis took place. The disagreement over the succession was kept out of the press, but it was a close run thing. In the early stages, for example, the professors felt they had to:

> correct an erroneous impression conveyed in your letter of 21st Instant, namely an intention on the part of your colleagues gratuitously and deliberately to insult you – your Colleagues protest against any such interpretation of their conduct – they deny having ever intended obtrusively to interfere with your rights or character.[20]

They were walking on eggshells and only averted disaster by calling on a wise court of directors to intervene.

When QCC opened to students in October 1849, there was no medical building and temporary accommodation managed by a single porter had to be arranged. The Earl of Clarendon, the lord lieutenant of the day, stepped in and funded the capital cost of what became the Clarendon Building. The medical school moved into it half way through the 1850/51 session. In November 1851, Alcock wrote to the President saying he now needed two porters, one to service Practical Anatomy (i.e., the dissecting laboratory) and one 'of a better class' to service his own professorial accommodation and museum. Two years later this letter would be included in a four-page public memorial to the Lord Lieutenant Sir George Grey, the Earl St Germans, in which Alcock sought to justify his actions. It was the tone as much as the content of his letters that so annoyed their recipients. For example, he ends this letter by saying:

> The Professor hopes the President will take immediate steps to place the department on a more suitable footing. The President, of course, has not forgotten, that at Cecelia-street, to which he is justly fond of referring, there were three – two porters for the Lecture department, and one, almost exclusively, for the Practical Anatomy. Is the Queen's College to be worse appointed than a proprietary school?[21]

Kane ignored the jibe and instructed the Registrar, Francis Albani, to reply on November 26 that the President had 'simplified the duties of the Medical porter' in order that his duties 'will be satisfactorily performed in the future'. This was dismissed with contempt by Alcock: 'Will it be believed that the SIMPLIFICATION here referred to was nothing less than leaving the Practical Anatomy, wholly, without attendance?'[22] He then complained to his Dean, Professor Fleming, Professor of Materia Medica, and posted a notice on the student notice board.[23] As the problem escalated, Kane consulted Robert Harrison, Professor of Anatomy in Trinity College Dublin, who replied in detail on 23 February 1852. On the central issue of portering, he said:

> there is <u>one</u> porter paid by the Board 20 Guineas per annum, apartments and coals – he attends the lecture room and museum and private rooms, cleans them, lights fires, rings the bell for each Professor (For all the Professors except of Chemistry in the Anatomical theatre): he gives some assistance and general superintendence in the dissecting room.

This was enough for Kane to hold the line. The Council believed Alcock had a big enough budget when his own fees were combined with the College provision. The Anatomy professor was paid 15 shillings by every medical student to defray the special costs of dissection. Alcock believed these fees were his own and were not to be used to subsidize his department. Kane knew that in other schools, including Trinity, they were used to fund the special costs of dissection. Alcock appealed to the first Triennial Visitation, which took place in May 1852. The Visitors ruled that Alcock was 'entitled to the fees, and to make such appointments as were necessary for his own profit'.[24] This was not an arbitration finding but a narrow legal interpretation of the position of the professor and while Kane had to accept it, he believed it failed to acknowledge the injustice suffered by Nathaniel Hobart, the lecturer Alcock had appointed.

According to Kane, Alcock only paid Hobart one-third of the students fees, even though Hobart delivered all of the lectures and dissections.[25] It was also Hobart's job to sign off on student attendance at Practical Anatomy. The Royal College of Surgeons in London required that the certificates of attendance at lectures should be signed by the professor and the certificates of attendance at Demonstrations and performance of Descriptive Anatomy should be signed by the teacher of those subjects (the professor could also sign if he wished) and that such certificates should also be signed by the dean of the Faculty of Medicine and countersigned by the Registrar.[26] Prior to the Visitors' decision, Alcock had withheld this certification in his stand-off with the President, so Kane had required Hobart to provide the certification. A further consequence of the decision in favour of Alcock was to remove the College element of Hobart's appointment and make him solely the employee of Alcock. During the summer of 1853:

> the fact of my appending my signature to the Anatomical certificates, at the desire of the College Authorities, was made the pretext by the Professor of Anatomy and Physiology for my 'abrupt and arbitrary' dismissal; though the certificates, without my signature, would have been quite useless to the candidates for the London Surgical Diploma, who were urgently demanding them at the time.[27]

The 'abrupt and arbitrary' expression quoted by Hobart was taken from Kane's third Annual Report made to Her Majesty as required by law. Such a public rebuke from the President added fuel to the fire of Alcock's interior demons and heralded the penultimate Act in the drama.

Having dismissed Hobart, and seen his successor resign – a man called Donegan – Alcock faced into the new academic year without an anatomical demonstrator. It was at this point that Alcock took his stand on principle, writing to Bullen in mid-October 1853 informing him:

> that a communication has been conveyed to me from Dr O'Connor that an arrangement has been made, under which subjects can be obtained from the Workhouse, without the privity or consent of the Guardians, if claimed by those requiring them in the capacity of relatives, and suggesting to me that I should obtain them thus, for the College. A similar communication and proposal have been made to me by Mr Gardiner another Medical officer of the Workhouse.
>
> It is unnecessary to observe to you that it would be contrary to the Anatomy Act to receive, possess or examine bodies thus obtained and that the party permitting and the party concerned in the examination would be liable to the penalties of the Act. Irrespective of these considerations I must therefore decline to be, in any way, a party to the proceeding. And as Doctor O'Connor's communication went to say, that certain other parties intended to obtain the subjects thus, I take leave to direct your attention officially to the matter, and to call upon you to adopt measures to prevent it, at least unless you are prepared to charge yourself with the responsibility as Inspector, or as a member of the Council to have recourse to this mode of supplying the College with subjects.[28]

This letter from Alcock placed him on a collision course with Denis Bullen, who, in forwarding Alcock's letter to the Castle, ended by stating:

> the personal imputations against Doctor O'Connor and myself conveyed in Doctor Alcock's letter addressed to an officer of the Crown are perfectly unjustifiable and I feel myself reluctantly obliged to claim the protection of the government and request to be permitted to decline receiving or noticing any such communications from Doctor Alcock in the future.

We do not know if the Chief Secretary bestowed upon Bullen 'the protection of the government' but Alcock's action and Bullen's response somehow set the seal on the final dénouement six months later.

Alcock did nothing further until the students complained and the College began to suffer reputational damage. According to Bullen 'several Medical students actually left the Queen's College in consequence of not finding subjects in the dissection room and went to follow their studies in other Schools'.[29] In November, 18 students sent a resolution to the President informing him:

> we have much reason to complain of the arrangements for supplying subjects and conducting the business of this department. We respectfully call your attention to this subject which is of such importance to our Medical Studies.[30]

The Medical Faculty were asked for their opinion. Reuben Harvey, Professor of Midwifery, presided as Dean. The other professors present were Bullen (Surgery), Alcock (Anatomy and Physiology) and O'Connor (Practice of Medicine). Bullen drafted two resolutions – the first that they were incompetent to rule on any complaint made against a professor as this could only be done by the President, and the second a motion of protest 'against the serious demand made upon their time in being required to consider the department of Practical Anatomy, over which the statutes give them no control'.[31] In a minority of one, Alcock voted against both. He did however, belatedly, apply to Bullen for subjects. Between 19 November and 13 December, nine dead bodies were supplied by the Inspector of Anatomy. These nine paupers, who unwittingly gave their bodies to the advancement of medical science under such fraught circumstances, were named in the Inspector's return for the quarter ended 31 December 1852 as:

Daniel O'Leary	aged 40	died of Bronchitis
Daniel Donovan	aged 60	died of Fever
John Bible	aged 14	died of Decline
James Harvey	aged 70	died of Dysentery
John Casey	aged 12	died of Enteritis
Margaret Higgins	aged 75	died of Asthma
Jane Callaghan	aged 80	died of Dysentery
Johanna O'Brien	aged 57	died of Asthma
Bess Buttimore	aged 22	died of Phthisis[32]

In December, the situation appeared to improve when the College Council sanctioned the appointment of the newly graduated Dr Walter Humphries as Alcock's assistant and Demonstrator in Practical Anatomy.[33] Kane did not approve but did not stand in the Council's way.[34] But more damage had been done to Alcock's fragile ego in that first term – his signature on the students' certificates was not recognized by the College of Surgeons in London. Their rule was that practical anatomy (i.e., dissection) could not be taught by the Professor of Anatomy and Physiology but had to be taught and signed off by a separate individual. The Professor could sign but his signature was irrelevant. This would have deeply humiliated Alcock because it made him dependent on a junior. To make matters worse, he received two letters dated 8 October and 15 November from William S. Gardiner, resident surgeon of the Cork Union Workhouse. With no demonstrator, Gardiner had to deal directly with Alcock and he did not find it easy. His two letters provide a real insight into the dilemma faced by the Workhouse doctors and the difficulty of dealing with Alcock at a personal level:

Dear Sir,

In reply to your note of the 6th October, I beg to state that I have already explained to you as clearly as I was able that the impediment which existed to the obtaining of subjects from this place did not originate with me, but arose from a prohibition given by some members of the House Committee which prohibition still exists, and of which you can satisfy yourself by application to the Master of the Work House.

As soon as the prohibition is removed, I shall, I assure you, be most happy to do what I can to accommodate you, as I think you must admit, I have done on former occasions, I cannot do so at present without violating the order from the House Committee.

I do not understand how you can state the cost of subjects as any difficulty in the way of dissection, as you are aware that the students would gladly pay a much larger sum, if they could be accommodated.

You may be assured that I should be as glad as you, that the matter was put on a more certain footing, as I must beg to remind you of the very great inconvenience and personal risk to which it has always exposed me. Yours Faithfully, W. S. Gardiner

My Dear Sir,

From the many difficulties I have, and the awful risk I run in my endeavour to procure subjects for you, along with the many shillings I have to give night watchmen and porters of this House to aid me in obtaining them, I find it wholly out of my power to remain to the proposition I made you in my last note, and now beg leave to inform you, that the only conditions on which I will have anything whatever to do in the business and undertake to insure you getting them, will be by your allowing me 15/= each for them, and sending me enclosed in an envelope this evening the sum of £6 which will cover the cost of 8 subjects, which if it be at all possible, I will procure for you – if not possible, I will again refund you the money.

Dr Caesar has always paid me beforehand for any subjects he has got, and has lately given me £1 for one, and is most anxious to get them at that rate, seeing the very great difficulty and hazard there is in my procuring them, so you should be very glad and not hesitate for a moment in acceding to the terms I now propose. Yours Faithfully, W. S. Gardiner.[35]

He found the payment of money particularly objectionable, believing that 'the Medical Officers of the Poor House have no right to impose a charge for anything done by them in the capacity of servants of the Board'.[36] Now he would have to pay and the cost was rising. Somehow he had to find a way out. From this point on, he increasingly sought deliverance in the law and its interpretation and in the end it would fail him.

Humphries was now in post and Alcock seemed willing to leave the business of dealing with the Inspector and the Workhouse to him. Bullen's returns to the Castle for the quarter ending 31 March 1853 show that ten subjects ranging in age from 5 years to 60 were sent to QCC, and four to Caesar's South Mall school, one of whom is simply 'A Child – name unknown'. His next return recorded six bodies to the South Mall school and none to QCC. The reason for this emerges later when he informed the Chief Secretary, Sir John Young, that:

> during the last academical session, the publication of certain correspondence in the newspapers respecting the Practical Anatomy department of the College alarmed some of the Guardians, who have given directions to the officials of the Workhouse to be cautious in their transacting with the College, lest the circumstances of taking the dead bodies of the paupers to the dissecting rooms may be made a matter of public discussion.[37]

This was the situation as the turbulent 1852/53 academic session drew to a close.

The students had gone for the summer but nothing was resolved. In July, Alcock complained to the Bursar that a valuable cranium had been stolen from his collection and another substituted in its place. Asked to attend on the Bursar and President to elaborate his charge, he refused. This brought back the vexed question of portering and the College's obligations to Alcock's private property. By the beginning of the next academic session – which would be his last – Alcock seems to have had not one friend among the medical fraternity of Cork. William Humphries, who of course was employed by Alcock, stuck by him and continued to bring his messages to the workhouse. That is all.

It might have been clear to any objective outsider that the only way the system was going to work was by playing the game that Bullen, the guardians and workhouse medical officers played, that, actually, everyone except Alcock played. The Board of Guardians were the legal custodians of the bodies. They were willing to turn a blind eye but if anything got out, the axe would fall and Gardiner might lose his job. O'Connor wrote in desperation that on two occasions the Board of Guardians 'instructed the Master to hand over unclaimed bodies for dissection, but as they did not wish to commit a resolution to writing, fearing it would get into the press, the Master does not wish to act'.[38] The workhouse medical officers were willing to facilitate the transfer of unclaimed bodies 'for facilitating this important branch of medical knowledge'–

and bodies were numerous: in some instances relatives did not have the money to bury them; in others, the relatives themselves had perished or emigrated.[39]

The second issue was the different roles of the Professor and the Inspector. Bullen saw his inspector role as talking confidentially to the guardians and ensuring that whatever money was necessary to oil the wheels of the dead carts changed hands as discretely as possible. He believed the professor should pay from the students' fees, and that the professor, through his demonstrator if necessary, should deal directly with the workhouse medical officers and dispose of the remains in consecrated ground as required by law. Professor Alcock saw it as the inspector's job to deliver subjects in whatever numbers and whenever required – at no cost. The stubbornness of both men sent anxiety levels in the workhouse through the roof, to the point where nobody really knew what to do and a kind of paralysis prevailed.

Bullen may have received some kind of green light from the Castle, if not from Alcock, because by the end of the quarter the Inspector had provided six bodies to QCC and four to the South Mall. It was now Bullen who was in control of the situation. All this time Alcock, with a favourable ruling by the Visitors to support him, was pursuing a legal action against the Bursar 'for the recovery of a fee for my lectures, which I am entitled, under 8 and 9 Vict.' He proposed to the Council that the matter 'be decided on a written case by the opinion of the Recorder, in order that public discussion might be avoided, but no notice has been taken of my letter.' So he continued to Larcom:

> I cannot therefore consider myself responsible for the consequences that may result from a public discussion, I have done all I could do without sacrificing what I believe to be my legal rights, to save the College from the possibility of injury.[40]

His next letter, this time to the Chief Secretary, lashed out at Bullen, who seemed to have become his particular animus:

> being at the same time Professor of Surgery in the College, and also the Dean of the Faculty and member of the Council, (he) must be supposed to understand and to appreciate the importance of this matter to the interests of the College, and who, in virtue of the authority with which, as Inspector, he has been invested by the Chief Secretary, must enjoy, and be able to exert an influence with, the Governors of Public Charities, which others cannot possess. For myself I shall be happy to facilitate this arrangement as far as may seem consistent with propriety.[41]

His last sentence, though qualified, appears to hint at a change of heart. On Christmas Eve, he wrote again expressing sadness that he was being 'charged with want of a cooperative spirit'.[42] His case against the Bursar was only instituted because the Visitors had ruled that his remedy was 'Action at Law for monies had and received'. 'The error into which I have fallen I trust will be excused'.[43] But it was too late for contrition. Young added a note to this letter that mentioned dismissal for the first time:

> Dr Alcock if not dismissed should not be allowed to continue at Cork. Whether his removal to Galway could be effected or not I cannot say, but it might be worthwhile to consider whether such removal or exchange could be effected and also on the whole if it would be judicious.[44]

Although Bullen had ceased to engage with Benjamin Alcock since the commencement of the 1853/54 academic year, Alcock continued to write to Bullen and his letters were duly forwarded to Larcom in Dublin Castle, unanswered save for the tersest acknowledgment. Meanwhile, Bullen continued to drip-feed bodies to prevent outright rebellion from the students while he awaited Government action. He claimed to Kane that Alcock had not agreed to relinquish control but that nevertheless, to prevent students from quitting the College and demanding a return of their fees, he had taken it upon himself to 'send in a few subjects for their immediate use'. He did this 'without my having any further communication with Professor Alcock' with the sole intention of averting 'irreparable injury' to the College, 'while government would have had time to make effectual regulations for conducting, in future, the department of Practical Anatomy'.[45] This seems to have been Bullen's code for coming to a decision about Alcock, a phrase he would repeat in different ways over the coming months.

The new year saw no let-up in the rising tension between the two men. On 6 January 1854 Alcock wrote:

> Sir, as the business of the Anatomical department will be resumed on Thursday next, I have to request that you will be so good as to order some subjects to be brought to the College. I shall feel obliged if you will also inform me whether you require any further funds.[46]

Bullen sent the letter back to Alcock with the following note on the same piece of paper:

> Sir, As the proceedings connected with the Practical Anatomy department of the Queen's College are under the consideration of the Government, before sending any more subjects to the College, I shall transmit your letter of 6th Inst to Sir Robert Kane.

The following day, Bullen forwarded the letter to Albani to pass on to the President and 'to enquire whether the Government have come to any decision with regard to the department of Practical Anatomy in the Queen's College'.[47]

Alcock meanwhile had written to John Bacot, Inspector of Anatomy for England, requesting details of the procedure followed there. He sent Bacot's reply to Sir John Young saying he would accept this in Cork. It was the one positive contribution Benjamin Alcock made in the entire controversy but by this stage it was far too late. He neutralized any positive effect six days later by laying before Young the legal opinion of John David FitzGerald of 1 Merrion Square, that confirmed that 'to obtain the subjects by claiming them, if untruly, in the capacity of a friend or relative – would constitute "a very serious misdemeanour"'.[48] Though legally, and we might say today, morally, correct, this was not what Sir John wanted to hear and he appears to have taken no action upon it.

At the end of the month of January, Kane advised Larcom that the Council had responded to his request 'to consider and report on the proper arrangements for supplying subjects to the Dissecting Students of the College'. The Council resolved 'that the external arrangements should be made by the Inspector of Anatomy and that the service necessary for the transport of the subjects to the College should be supplied by the College Authorities'. Kane added that in his own experience, transport costs were paid by the student fees and supervised by the Professor of Anatomy. The Council resolution had carefully avoided any mention of the Professor's role. It seems Alcock still had friends among his colleague professors but Kane was not letting their ambiguity pass without comment.

Denis Bullen was not among Alcock's allies. His final thrust was a letter sent to the President on 22 February and forwarded to Larcom three days later. To understand the full force of this, it is necessary first to retrace our steps to 6 January when Alcock wrote to Humphries, his hapless assistant, asking him to confirm the accuracy of Alcock's description of the proposal made by O'Connor back in mid-October. At that time, Alcock had written to Humphries declining:

> to have anything to do with the arrangement, communicated to you by Drs Bullen and O'Connor, which you were authorized to convey to me – that I should obtain the subjects from the Poor House by claiming them in the capacity of friend of the deceased.

Humphries confirmed the accuracy of the letter, except for one point – it was O'Connor's suggestion alone, Bullen had not been party to it. Why would he need to confirm the accuracy of his letter? The explanation comes in Bullen's letter of 22 February. Having repeatedly stressed that he could only do his job if confidentiality were respected, he revealed the following:

> This day, however, a communication has been made to me by the Medical Officers of the Workhouse intimating that Mr Richard Jameson, the Poor Law Guardian who has hitherto taken the most active part in preventing

dead bodies being taken from the Workhouse for Anatomical purposes, called upon Mr Wm Gardiner, the resident surgeon, and warned him not to allow dead bodies to be removed because Doctor Alcock had waited on him, and placed in his hands the confidential letters, which had passed between Wm. Gardiner and Dr Alcock regulating the arrangements, by which the subjects had been transferred from the Workhouse to the College.

Under these circumstances, you will, I am sure, admit the impossibility of my continuing to furnish the Queen's College with subjects, until such time as the Government shall have come to some conclusion in reference to the several matters connected with the Practical Anatomy department, which are, at present, under consideration.[49]

Six days later, the axe fell: Alcock received a letter from Larcom requiring his resignation.[50] He held out until 14 March 1854 when he wrote to Edward Granville, Earl St Germans, Lord Lieutenant of Ireland:

My Lord,

Not having received the honour of a reply to my letter of the 6th inst. I am reluctantly led to the conclusion that your Excellency's determination has undergone no change.

I therefore beg leave respectfully to tender to your Excellency my resignation of the professorship, which I have held in Queen's College Cork. And at the same time, in the most respectful manner, to convey to Your Excellency the deep sense which I entertain of the courtesy and consideration, which you have been pleased to extend to me in this matter.[51]

Alcock made several attempts to regain his chair, including sending a lengthy memorial to the Queen on 28 April 1855.[52] It was referred by the Home Secretary, Sir George Grey, to the government in Ireland and the Lord Lieutenant had refused to consider it. He wrote directly to Grey on 14 July, again with no result. He also wrote to the local and medical press complaining of the unjust way he had been treated.[53] He wrote a final memorial to the Lord Lieutenant on 3 September 1858.[54] It was all to no avail. In 1859 he left the country for America and never returned.

The story of Benjamin Alcock at Queen's College Cork is a tragic one. Bullen seems to have played a Machiavellian role by ceasing meaningful communication with Alcock and sending all his letters to Dublin Castle. When he took control of the bodies, he drip fed them so as to prolong the controversy and let Alcock dig himself deeper into trouble. He kept pressing for a 'decision from government' and finally, informed on Alcock's treachery in betraying the confidence of the workhouse medical officers. This appears an extraordinary act of sabotage on Alcock's part. The kindest interpretation would be that he was so outraged that nobody would take the Anatomy Act seriously that he picked the one man who he believed would. But it shows also that his priority was no longer the good of the College, or his Department, or even himself. He seemed rather to be seeking his own destruction. Yet this is belied by his spirited defence of his chair and his subsequent pleadings to the Chief Secretary for redress and an alternative appointment that never came. Perhaps the nearest we can get is the oblique reference of his niece Dorothy who spoke of her grandfather, Alcock's father, as generating 'filial fear' in his sons. It may have been less wholesome than she would have us believe.

Up to now, nobody seems to have looked into what happened to Alcock after he emigrated. He doesn't even have a recorded date of death. Recent research using on-line genealogy tools has revealed that he settled in Steuben County in up-state New York. He married another Irish immigrant whose first name was Sarah (family name unknown) and Sarah already had a daughter called Ellen. They settled in Hammondsport, which was at the centre of a wine growing area, and the Alcocks bought a three-acre site where they grew grapes for Hammondsport's wine industry. Benjamin died in 1865 and left his estate to Ellen. She married a reverend gentleman called Daniel Loveridge and eventually they moved to Eugene, Oregon, where she died in 1903. Sarah survived Benjamin by thirteen years, and made a good living out of grapes. She is buried beside her husband less than a hundred meters from their home. Like many an emigrant before and after him, Alcock seems to have found a measure of restoration and redemption in his new home.[55]

At first sight Bullen emerged the clear winner. He had engineered the removal of a troublesome professor and covered his tracks reasonably well in the process. Kane had survived too, at least until the next round in the contest of the President vs. the Professors, which was not long in coming. Their champion on this occasion would be George Boole, an altogether more rooted individual with a strong ethical sense of right and wrong.[56] But what had the victory cost Denis Brenan Bullen? The price, and it was ultimately a heavy one, was the hardening of a proud personality into something more calculating and ruthless that would eventually lead to his undoing. To see how this developed we need to turn again to Henry Augustus Caesar, proprietor of the Cork School of Medicine on the South Mall.

5. Caesar

Henry Augustus Caesar (1800–65) has received but incidental attention from historians, mainly in connection with the scramble for chairs in Queen's College Cork in 1848 and again in 1854 when the Anatomy chair became vacant for a second time. His supporters appear in the cloud of suspects that emerged after the fire that burnt down the West Wing of the College on the night of 15 May 1862, 'parties ... who felt angered at the suppression of Dr Cosar's establishment'.[1] Over the next decade he emerges as Bullen's main protagonist, implacable in defending his school and resisting all attempts by the Inspector to close it.

We know from a letter written by Andrew Roche, Mayor of Cork, that was included in Caesar's testimonials for the Queen's College chair in 1847 that the two were friends as early as 1824. Caesar was President of the Cork Medico-Chirurgical Society before he left to study in Edinburgh where he had had a distinguished student career, being twice elected President of the Hunterian Medical Society of Edinburgh.[2] He began lecturing in Anatomy in 1828, initially from Rutland Street and later from rooms at the back of his house on South Mall. He married 21-year-old Prudence Thompson in 1831 who bore him a large family. In 1848 he correctly predicted that it would in a short time be overshadowed by QCC's medical school.[3] In 1854, he offered to bring his private school with him if he were appointed Professor of Anatomy and Physiology.[4] As an Anglican, he prided himself on his sensitivity to Catholicism and his friendly relations with his Catholic colleagues and students.[5] This was an important bonus for his school at a time when religious allegiance was a source of tension and prejudice.

He put considerable money into developing the Cork School of Medicine on the South Mall. In 1836, after lecturing for six or seven years, he boasted a 'New Anatomical Theatre' with 'strong clear light from the top', and 'fitted up with every attention to comfort, convenience and instruction'.[6] Six years later, he added a 'new lecture room, dissecting room, museum, laboratory'.[7] After Wherland closed his school in 1844, Caesar's school became the only medical school in the city until Queen's College opened its doors in 1849. Those who had lectured with Woodroffe and Wherland moved to the South Mall school, which for a few short years became quite renowned.[8] Caesar never ran into the animosity directed at Woodroffe by the populace of Cork who, by the mid-1840s, were perhaps inured to rowdy medical students, unpleasant odours and carts shuffling in and out of the school gates at early hours of the morning.

He seems to have been sufficiently respected in the city to have weathered the storms of grave robbing, the Poor Law, the Famine and even the advent of QCC. However, the one person against whom his ecumenical spirit seems to have utterly failed him was the Inspector of Anatomy.

We have already noted a preliminary skirmish in 1851 when Caesar was reported to Dublin Castle for not filing quarterly returns. At about the same time he had sought approval from Dublin Castle for a teacher of operative surgery named Cotter, newly arrived in Cork from Paris. His letter to the Castle ended 'Doctor Cotter further hopes that the decision will not be left to the Inspector of Anatomy of Cork'.[9] Of course Bullen was informed by the Castle and actually raised no objection, but the very fact that Caesar tried to avoid him is indicative of their poor professional relationship. However, the glowing embers of hostility burst into flames of open conflict when the Anatomy Inspector made an unannounced visit to Caesar's school on 21 November 1857 and found 'a female subject partly dissected; no certificate regarding this body was transmitted to me'.[10] Bullen claimed this was not an isolated case but had been going on for twelve months. In his usual way, he had reported it to Government and 'sent the Secretary's letter to Dr Caesar'. Caesar then produced 'notice for the body' but 'I did not receive that as a certificate' claimed the Inspector. Caesar's response was that he had used the same procedure for many years, which was to send the certificates all together 'at the end of the season instead of transmitting them one by one'. This was not strictly in accordance with the Act which required quarterly returns but Bullen did not deny that it was the procedure followed. Bullen's report to government has not survived but the name of the subject has. His return for 31 December 1857 recorded three subjects delivered to the South Mall School: Edward Barry, aged 41 of Queenstown who died of phthisis on 27 October, Catherine Magrath, aged 36 of the General Union who died of phthisis on 29 October and James Regan, aged 36 who died of phthisis (date not recorded). The body on the table must have been that of Catherine Magrath, the only female of the three. Gardiner's entry to the dead book states Edward Barry died of bronchitis aged 55 and Catherine Magrath died of erysipelas aged 40. Bullen's returns of a year before, i.e., 31 December 1856, show nine subjects dissected in the South Mall school but in 1857, no reports were made between January and June. Caesar may have had another supplier but if this was so, he did not tell the Inspector. It could have been the South Infirmary.

The other possibility is that Bullen used his influence in the Cork Workhouse to cut off supply. The Inspector persuaded the government to take a case against Caesar for infringement of the Anatomy Act. The initial hearing of the *Queen vs. H.A. Caesar* took place on Thursday 3 December 1857.[11] The case seems to have been built on evidence from the Inspector that members of the County Club nearby had been 'annoyed by an unwholesome odour of the burning of human bones which took place within the school' and that 'there had been a total cessation of anatomical studies in the school, and that but one human body (the luckless Catherine Magrath), had been received for dissection within a given period' (1857).[12] In a second letter to the Chief Secretary he stated that, 'notwithstanding the total cessation of anatomical studies, certificates of attendance of the pupils at lectures, which had not been delivered, had been sent to the London College'.[13] As a result of his letter, the College of Surgeons in London withdrew its recognition of Caesar's school on 10 May 1860.[14] Caesar refused to accept this, and brought a suit against Bullen for libel by the contents of these letters. His attorney was Charles Henry Woodroffe, eldest son of John, and by this time one of the most successful barristers in the country. The hearings began in 1862 and dragged on over the succeeding two years. The last report appears in July 1864 when the hearing was adjourned 'till next term'.

This law suit laid bare the animosity between these two men. At one point Bullen claimed Caesar was in 'embarrassed circumstances' long before the RCSE withdrew recognition of his certificates, such that he would not be able to pay for the trial and because he resided in England, he should have to provide security for costs.[15] Bullen seems to have won that particular round. The other remarkable thing is that Caesar kept placing annual advertisements in the newspapers announcing the start of the forthcoming academic sessions each year between 1857/8 and 1864/5. The notice for the 1858/9 session must have particularly incensed Bullen, assuring his readers 'its supply of subjects is unlimited and students may depend on having the same zeal evinced for their instruction which has characterized it for over thirty years'.[16] How do we square this with Bullen's evidence that tuition had ceased and the supply of bodies had dried up? The only explanation that makes sense is that Caesar did indeed have an alternative supply and may have conducted clandestine dissection classes in the school or used post mortem examinations in the South Infirmary. O'Connor claimed in 1853 that Caesar 'in consequence of the good feeling entertained towards him in this City and County, would legally obtain subjects from other institutions besides the Workhouse'.

We actually have a reference dated November 1863 written by Caesar for a student called Cleophas William Seaborne who went on to get his Licentiate from Glasgow and his MD from St Andrews. It reads:

> I am happy to bear testimony to the moral demeanour, and anxious assiduity with which Dr Seaborne conducted himself for the two years which he studied in the Cork School of Medicine, and attended the Medical and Surgical practice of the North and South Infirmaries, and am well aware his indefatigable industry obtained for him the marked attention of all his teachers'.[17]

All this suggests that Caesar refused to close his school and defied all attempts by the Inspector of Anatomy to make him do so, including withdrawal of his licence, hard fought for back in 1834, and withdrawal of recognition of his certificates by the RCSE. It goes a long way in explaining his reaction to Bullen's disgrace after the QCC fire.

The West Wing fire that blazed with such fury in May 1862 has already been referred to at the beginning of this chapter. It has been discussed in detail by John A. Murphy in his history of the College.[18] Just two aspects concern us here, the disgrace of Denis Brenan Bullen and Caesar's response to it.

Bullen had ambitions to be President and Sir Robert Kane had apparently had enough by 1862. He had become deeply disillusioned by the hostility of the Catholic Church but the immediate cause of his anger was a Commons motion from John Pope Hennessy MP against his double jobbing, which was a continuing source of friction between the President and his professors.[19] The two men had had a conversation on the evening of the fire that Bullen subsequently recorded in his diary or 'commonplace book':

> It struck me that Sir Robert Kane intended to use influence with Sir Robert Peel, and induce the Chief Secretary to make some strong demonstration against the Ultramontanes, the result of which would render it an impossibility ever to effect an amicable settlement of the educational questions in dispute between Lord Palmerston's Ministry and the Roman Catholic members of Parliament. Acting under this impression, I hurried home, prepared and forwarded by that evening's mail the following communication to the Lord Lieutenant.[20]

The communication was his bid for the presidency, which Kane had told him he was about to relinquish. However, the fire changed everything for Kane. Resignation under such circumstances would have been interpreted by his enemies as an admission of guilt or weakness. Four days later, the two men had a further conversation in which Bullen claimed the president had proposed they both collaborate in a report to government that blamed the fire on 'ultramontane influence'. Bullen's contemporaneous notes of these conversations were quite possibly true – Kane's bitter anti-church feelings, though a Catholic, were well known and as Bullen said on another occasion 'We all know there is a freemasonry in professions, which ought to be held sacred'. Kane, who was also a medical man, may well have felt he was speaking to a friend and colleague within that freemasonry.

However, a year later, with Kane still in post, all had changed. Prompted by some articles Kane had sent to the Cork papers, Bullen did what he had done many times in his career; he turned everything over to Dublin Castle stating that he was prepared to state under oath that 'the incendiary is an official of the College and that the conduct of Sir Robert Kane with reference thereto demands inquiry'.[21] Contemporaneously he briefed John Pope Hennessy MP who told the Commons that a QCC professor had declared there was strong circumstantial evidence to suggest that the fire was the work of a College official.[22] Bullen's name was revealed as a result of pressure from Kane himself who hotly denied everything and, crucially, was backed in doing so by Dublin Castle. The matter was raised at the triennial visitation. With no corroborating evidence, Bullen totally withdrew his accusation claiming he had been mistaken and that the passage of time had left 'an erroneous impression' of what had passed between himself and the President. It was the first time in his career that Bullen had failed to stand over what he had said. We recalled above his earlier words about a professional freemasonry. That sentence continued 'and that he who violates that freemasonry, in so doing reflects very little honour either upon himself individually, or upon the profession to which he belongs'. In this context, it was both a failed political gambit and a betrayal of confidential conversations. Faced with that betrayal, Kane had no alternative but to deny everything and fight for his good name; but the other betrayal was of Bullen himself. For his whole career he had looked for and found a ready ear from the authorities in Dublin Castle for his communications as Inspector of Anatomy. He may have counted on a continuation of this support. The most likely arsonist was the College steward, William Williams, who was known to be in the president's confidence. If Williams was the culprit, then indeed Kane would have had questions to answer. If the Castle had agreed, then no corroborating evidence would have been required – but it didn't agree. After standing behind Sir Robert Kane against the bishops who had boycotted the new colleges, such an appalling vista was too much for the Castle to contemplate.

So having assiduously cultivated friendships with senior Castle officials throughout his career, Bullen suddenly found he had none. His own account of events suggests a combination of over-confidence and impulsiveness in his character set in train a series of events that spiralled out of control. On the day his letter of retraction was read out, his sacking became inevitable. George Boole, QCC Professor of Mathematics, was among those who realized this intuitively. Mary Boole tells us that as Bullen left the Aula Maxima, Boole walked up to him and offered him his arm. Referring to her husband, she then observes that 'I believe he suffered far more than the culprit himself did'. She adds a final sentence to her letter that 'During his last illness, as soon as it became desirable to call in a second physician, he selected the dismissed professor'.[23] It seems that Richard Barter, Boole's regular physician, gave up his attendance on 4 December 1864, four days before Boole's death, in favour of Bullen who was 'within a minute's call'. Barter's reason was that 'the idle pantomime of two physicians attending, who will not meet or act together,* must render their professional services worse than useless'. The asterisk refers to a footnote which reads 'I never expressed the slightest unwillingness to meet Dr Bullen, the objection coming entirely from his side!'[24] We do not have Bullen's side of this controversial footnote but Barter felt sufficiently strongly about it to seek to justify himself in print.

On 10 May, Bullen was formally dismissed from his chair by a letter from the Home Office delivered by the hand of Sir Robert Kane. Henry Caesar was less magnanimous than George Boole. The man who had prided himself on his good relations with his Catholic students and friends took revenge within days of Bullen's dismissal. Although we do not have the correspondence, the dates and annotations of the CSORP index tell the tale.

> CSORP annotated index, 1864
> *Dr Caesar 12 May – that Dr Bullen be removed from Inspectorship of Anatomy*
> (On 16 May, William Beamish was appointed Inspector of Anatomy for the Province of Munster. Caesar wrote on the same day asking for his licence back.)
> *Dr Caesar 16 May – for licence for bodies for Anatomy*
> *Dr Caesar 21 May – School of Anatomy Cork*
> *Dr Caesar 24 May – Further Practice of Anatomy*
> *Dr Bullen 2 July – Proceedings against him by Dr Caesar*
> *Dr Caesar 25 July – further for compensation for loss of school*
> *Dr Caesar 19 Dec. – For renewal of licence*

An advertisement appeared in the *Southern Reporter* dated 2 July 1864 stating that:

> Dr Caesar will commence the Second Section of his Lectures on the Muscular, Vascular, and Nervous Systems, with relative, regional and Surgical Anatomy on TUESDAY, 7th FEBRUARY next, which Gentlemen who attended the Ostiological Part of the course last Session are invited to attend, in order that they may be entitled to their Certificates, the then Inspector of Anatomy having refused to allow subjects.

So it seems that after a professional career during which Caesar had first kept his distance from the Inspector and then enjoined him (one might almost say) in mortal combat, Caesar came out the victor, but it was a short-lived and bitter sweet victory. He never delivered his lectures on the muscular, vascular and nervous system. In January, his son, John Caesar, fell victim to the typhus epidemic then sweeping the city. He had been tending fever patients in the Southern Auxiliary Fever Hospital. Considerable controversy surrounded John Caesar's death which some laid at the door of the Poor Law Guardians for not providing him with an assistant.[25] Then, on 27 March, Caesar himself died. His death certificate records dysentery as the cause of death, lasting 'a few weeks'. The *Cork Examiner*'s death notice said 'after a lengthened illness'.[26] We do not know what this implied but it may help explain the haste with which he sought to re-establish his school after Bullen's disgrace.

Bullen too lost a son, though not by death. Dr Francis Brenan Bullen resigned from his post in the North Infirmary in August 1865 and emigrated to make a new and successful career in Ballarat Free Hospital, Australia.[27] Nathaniel Hobart was elected without opposition in his place, finally securing a hospital position in the city.[28]

The disgraced Bullen, now dismissed as Inspector of Anatomy, was extended a helping hand by his old friend, Denis O'Connor, in 'giving the benefit of his experience in consultation' at the Mercy Hospital which he continued to do till his death on 25 March 1866.[29] His death certificate records the cause of death as capillary bronchitis and failing heart. He survived Caesar by less than a year.

Later in 1866, another row blew up over the transport of bodies from the Cork Workhouse to QCC. The House Committee was asked to investigate an accusation that some bodies had been transported 'in a state of nudity ... covered with a piece of mat'. It found that the statement was 'founded on fact' and recommended that:

> the practice if allowed to continue should be subject to better regulations than those existing at present; that your Committee ask for full power to communicate with the College authorities, and make further arrangements on the subject.[30]

It was a five-man committee of guardians chaired by the High Sheriff, Thomas Lyons. The fifth man was none other than Dr James Wherland who had tried and failed to secure the Chair of Anatomy and Physiology in QCC. The personnel may have changed but the issues remained the same. However on each occasion the outcry became more muted till eventually, well into the new century, voluntary donations entirely replaced the unclaimed bodies of the poor. So who were the real victims of Warburton's flawed and ambiguous legislation in nineteenth-century Cork? The destitute and their families certainly top the list – but they were not the only ones.

Conclusion

Denis Bullen's life began contemporaneously with the Napoleonic wars and ended as the American Civil War drew to a close, almost exactly coinciding with the first two-thirds of the 19th century. He had witnessed the culmination of the industrial revolution, the invention of the railways, photography, the expansion of the British Empire, the opening up of Australia, and closer to his own areas of interest, the discovery of vaccination and anaesthesia. In his own career, his great achievements were the reinvigoration of the North Infirmary and his role, whatever that truly was, in the founding of Queen's College Cork. Throughout most of his career he had been a dedicated supporter of medical education and had probably done more than any other single individual to foster its growth in his native city. His dismissal from QCC has cast a shadow over what was otherwise a fine career. George Boole's gesture in offering his arm as Bullen left the Aula Maxima in disgrace seems to acknowledge this.

On the other hand, he was never far from controversy. His self-confidence bordered on arrogance and his response to Benjamin Alcock, while certainly not the easiest of academic colleagues, was harsh and calculating. His approach to Alcock and Caesar was almost entirely based on the exercise of power and influence with Dublin Castle. Perhaps this is what was behind Mary Boole's assessment that her husband 'suffered far more than the culprit himself did'. In Robert Kane he met his match. Kane was able to wield power himself and whatever his opinions of the mandarins of Dublin Castle, he was more than able to keep them on his side when it counted.

There is little in the record that speaks of Bullen's clinical skill as a practising surgeon or a teacher of surgery. We find occasional references to court appearances as an expert witness but unlike Caesar we have no tributes from past pupils. When applying for the Chair at QCC he made much of his papers on cholera written after the epidemic of 1832 but he seems to have taken no part in the medical or indeed literary societies in Cork which were active in the middle decades of the century. In the controversy over the siting of the Workhouse, he did not, like O'Connor, speak from a knowledge of the lives of the poor in that area. We do however have the evidence of Sarah Atkinson that, with his father, he provided dedicated and gratuitous care to the newly founded Sisters of Charity. In the wider scheme of things, his forceful character dominated the medical life of the city throughout the greater part of seven tumultuous decades.

Notes

ABBREVIATIONS

AH	Apothecaries' Hall
CC	*Cork Constitution, or Cork Advertiser*
CDR	*Cork Daily Reporter*
CE	*Cork Examiner*
CSOOP	NAI Chief Secretary's Office Official Papers
CSORP	NAI Chief Secretary's Office Registered Papers
DIB	*Dictionary of Irish biography*
DMP	*Dublin Medical Press*
FJ	*Freeman's Journal*
JCHAS	*Journal of the Cork Historical and Archaeological Society*
LR	*Limerick Reporter*
MD	Doctor of Medicine
NAI	National Archives of Ireland
NLI	National Library of Ireland
NUIG	National University of Ireland, Galway
ODNB	*Oxford dictionary of national biography*
Parl. Debs.	Parliamentary Debates
QCC	Queen's College Cork
RCI	Royal Cork Institution
RCSE	Royal College of Surgeons in England
RCSI	Royal College of Surgeons in Ireland
SN	*Saunders Newsletter*
SR	*Southern Reporter and Cork Daily Commercial Courier*
TNA	The National Archives of England and Wales
UCC	University College Cork
WM	*Waterford Mail*

INTRODUCTION

1 Minutes of the Trustees of the South Infirmary, 19 Aug. 1813. Courtesy of the South Infirmary/Victoria University Hospital.

2 Neil Cronin, *The medical profession and the exercise of power in early nineteenth-century Cork,* Maynooth Studies in Local History, 115 (Dublin, 2014).

3 Cronin, *The medical profession,* p. 7.

4 Bull was appointed to this position ahead of George Howe in February 1820. The need for this post is evidence of Woodroffe's success in increasing the numbers of surgical patients at the South Infirmary (Minutes of the Trustees).

5 Cronin, *The medical profession,* p. 21.

6 Ruth Richardson, *Death, dissection and the destitute* (London, 1987).

7 Michael Hanna and Julie Crowe, 'What happened to Benjamin Alcock?', *JCHAS,* 125 (2020), pp 50–64.

8 Denis Charles O'Connor, *Seventeen years' experience of workhouse life* (Dublin, 1861).

9 Colman O'Mahony, *Cork's Poor Law palace workhouse life, 1838–1890* (Cork, 2005).

10 Ronan O'Rahilly, *A history of Cork Medical School 1849–1949* (Cork, 1949).

11 John A. Murphy, *The College: a history of Queen's/University College Cork, 1845–1995* (Cork, 1995).

12 CSOOP 1854/61.

13 Murphy, *The College*.
14 *CE*, 29 Mar. 1865.

I. EARLY SUCCESSES

1   Helen Andrews, 'Bullen, Denis Brenan' in James McGuire and James Quinn (eds), *Dictionary of Irish biography* (Cambridge, 2009). (dib.cambridge.org)
2   http:/www.thepeerage.com/p35669. htm#i356681 quoted in Cronin, *The medical profession*, p. 13.
3   Sarah Atkinson, *Mary Aikenhead: her life, her work, and her friends* (Dublin, 1879).
4   Cronin, *The medical profession*, p. 14.
5   William Bullen, Letter to T. Lane, 25 Sept. 1846, TCD/MS 873/198.
6   Cronin, *The medical profession*, p. 63.
7   Atkinson, *Mary Aikenhead*, p. 100.
8   J.S. Crowley, R.J.N. Devoy, D. Linehan, P. O'Flanagan (eds), *Atlas of Cork city* (Cork, 2005), pp 223–5.
9   *Royal Commission on Irish Education, Seventh Report, Appendix (Cork)* (London, 1827), HC (443), xiii, p. 22.
10 Michael Hanna, 'John Woodroffe MD: a pioneer of medical education', *JCHAS*, 120 (2015), p. 23.
11 John Woodroffe, *Observations on Dr Bullen's Letter to the Trustees of the South Infirmary* (Cork, 1820), p. 55.
12 Ibid., p. 49.
13 National Portrait Gallery, https://www. npg.org.uk/collections/search/person/ mp06131/george-russell-dartnell
14 Honor de Pencier, author of *Posted to Canada – the watercolours of George Russell Dartnell 1835–1844* (Toronto and Oxford, 1987), personal communication of Dartnell's certificates.
15 Sir James Alexander, *l'Acadie; or Seven years explorations in British America* (London, 1849), vol. 1, pp 201–14.
16 *CC*, 15 Nov. 1827.
17 CSORP 1825 12767.
18 Ibid.
19 *CC*, 28 Feb. 1826.
20 Cronin, *The medical profession*, p. 50.
21 *SR*, 18 Nov. 1838.
22 CSOOP, Series 2, 1832–1880 – OP 1849 124.
23 *First Report of Her Majesty's Commissioners for enquiring into the conditions of the poorer classes of Ireland: Appendix B*, HC 1835 (369), pp 54–7.

24 Karen Sonnelitter, *Charity movements in eighteenth-century Ireland: philanthropy and improvement* (Suffolk and New York, 2016), p. 79.
25 *Poorer classes in Ireland*, Appendix B, p. 364.
26 Ibid., p. 366
27 *Select Committee on Medical Charities in Ireland together with Minutes of Evidence, Appendix and Index*. HC 1843 (412), x, p. 234.
28 Cork City Archives, *Minute book of the Committee of Merchants*, Meeting of 30 Aug. 1794.
29 R. Gordon, *Estimates, Miscellaneous Services, 1840–41 (I.-V.)*, HC 1840 (179), xxx, pp 12–16. This document also links Henrique and Antonio Sampayo.
30 Hazard's *Register of Pennsylvania*, XIII, 4, pp 60–1.
31 *CC*, 28 July 1829.
32 *SR*, 23 Oct. 1832.
33 *SR*, 26 Oct. 1833.
34 Ibid.
35 Louis Perrin et al., *Report of the Commissioners appointed to inquire into the Municipal Corporations (Ireland)*, HC 1835 (23–25, 27, 28), xxvii p. 56.
36 *Select Committee on Medical Charities in Ireland*, p. 235.
37 *SN*, 11 May 1859.
38 *CE*, 28 Nov. 1866.

2. THE ANATOMY ACT

1   James Elwick, *Styles of reasoning in the British life sciences: shared assumptions, 1820–58* (London and New York, 2007), p. 21.
2   C.S. Breathnach, 'Barry, Sir David (1780–1835), army surgeon and physiologist', *ODNB*.
3   Henry Warburton, *Select Committee to inquire into the Manner of obtaining Subjects for Dissection in Schools of Anatomy. Report, Minutes of Evidence, Appendix*. HC 1828, (568), vii, p. 55.
4   Ibid., p. 52.
5   Helen Andrews, 'Macartney, James', *DIB*.
6   *Select Committee to inquire into Schools of Anatomy*, p. 106.
7   William Burke and William Hare, of Irish birth but living in Edinburgh, murdered 10 victims in 1828, passing

these bodies on to Robert Knox, Professor of Surgery at the University of Edinburgh, for dissection; Knox paid between £8 and £10 for each body. The two were arrested on 3 Nov. 1828. Hare turned King's evidence and his testimony condemned Burke to a guilty verdict on Christmas Day, 1828. He was hanged on 28 January 1829 and his body was dissected. Knox was not convicted of any crime.

8   John Bishop and Thomas Williams were arrested just over three years after Burke and Hare, tried at the Old Bailey on 2–3 Dec. and hanged on 5 Dec. 1831.

9   *Select Committee to inquire into Schools of Anatomy*, p. 107.

10 Helen MacDonald, *Procuring corpses: the English anatomy inspectorate, 1842 to 1858* (London, 2009).

11 *HC Deb.* (11 Apr. 1832). Series 3, vol. 10, cols. 316–22.

12 2 Will. IV.–Sess. 1831–2. *A bill [as amended on re-commitment] for regulating schools of anatomy*, HC (201) i. p. 2.

13 2 Will. IV.–Sess. 1831–2. *A bill [as amended on the second re-commitment] for regulating schools of anatomy*, (HC) (419) i. p. 3.

14 Ibid., p. 4.

15 Linde Lunney, 'Murray, Sir James' in *DIB*.

16 CSORP, 1836, 277.

17 TNA, MH 74 15; Bacot to Ellis, 14 Oct. 1857, p. 453, cited in Helen MacDonald, *Procuring corpses*.

18 CSORP, 1860, 17625; South to Larcom, 26 July 1860.

19 The numbers were RCSI (83); Carmichael School (46); Dr Steevens' School (29); the Catholic University (40); Ledwich School (73) and Trinity College (29).

20 CSORP, 1850, H2007; Murray to Somerville, 22 Mar. 1850.

21 CSORP, 1833, 318.

22 Ibid., Caesar to Lord Morpeth, 20 Nov, 14 Dec., 30 Dec. 1834.

23 *Select Committee on Diocesan and Foundation Schools, and System of Education in Ireland. Report, Minutes of Evidence, Appendix Part 1*, HC 1835 (630), xiii, p. 329.

24 CSORP, 1835, 1018.

25 *The medical directory for Ireland 1852*, p. 103.

26 CSOOP, 1849, 124.

27 Ibid.

3. THE BEST OF TIMES, THE WORST OF TIMES

1   Lawrence M. Geary, *Medicine and charity in Ireland, 1718–1851* (Dublin, 2004), p. 157.

2   Ibid., p. 158.

3   Ibid., p. 159.

4   *Select Committee on Medical Charities in Ireland*, p. 237.

5   Ibid.

6   Ibid., p.238.

7   *Select Committee on Medical Charities in Ireland*, p. 239.

8   *SR*, 12 Sept. 1843.

9   *Select Committee on Medical Charities in Ireland, 1843*, p. 240.

10 Ibid.

11 Colman O'Mahony, *Cork's Poor Law palace*, pp 293–4.

12 Denis Charles O'Connor, *Seventeen years' experience of workhouse life* (Dublin, 1861), p. 58.

13 G.D. Burtchaell and T.U. Sadlier, *Alumni Dublinenses* (London, 1924), p. 630.

14 CSOOP, 1849, 124.

15 Cathy Hayes, 'O'Connor, Denis Charles', *DIB*.

16 *SR*, 13 Oct. 1838; *SR*, 12 Oct. 1839; *SR*, 17 Oct. 1840; *CE*, 22 Oct. 1841; *CE*, 28 Oct. 1842; *SR*, 28 Oct. 1843.

17 Cork City and County Archives, BG/69/A, *Board of Guardians Minutes Books*, Book 1, Minutes of 27 July 1840, p. 93.

18 Ibid., p. 80.

19 *Minute Book of the Cork County and City Medical and Surgical Society*. Courtesy of Dr Margaret O'Connor. O'Connor and Popham were among six members asked to prepare rules for the society.

20 Cathy Hayes, 'O'Connor, Denis Charles', *DIB*.

21 Thomas Holt, *Plan of the city and suburbs of Cork, 1832.*

22 *SR*, 25 July 1840.

23 *Select Committee on Medical Charities in Ireland*, p. 241.

24 Cork City and County Archives, BG/69/A, *Cork Board of Guardians Minute Books, Book 3*, 6 Mar. 1843.

25 Ibid., *Book 1*, 15 July 1839.
26 *SR*, 2 Apr. 1840.
27 *SR*, 4 Apr. 1840.
28 Cork City and County Archives, BG/69/A, *Cork Board of Guardians Minute Books, Book 1*, 6 Apr., 1840.
29 *LR*, 10 Feb. 1843.
30 Roger Herlihy, *Tales from Victorian Cork, 1837–1859* (Cork, 2012), pp 34–6.
31 Ibid.
32 *WM*, 10 Aug. 1831.
33 *HC Deb.* (9 May 1845). Series 3, vol. 80, cols. 342–413.
34 *SR*, 22 May 1845.
35 CSOOP, 1849, 124.
36 Ibid.
37 CSOOP, 1849, 124.
38 Ibid.
39 Ibid.
40 *CE*, 20 Sept. 1866.
41 Atkinson, *Mary Aikenhead*, p. 358.
42 Ibid., p. 364.
43 *CE*, 9 Mar. 1846.
44 *SR*, 5 Apr. 1849.
45 Cork City and County Archives, BG/69/A, *Cork Board of Guardians Minute Books, Book 6*, p. 95.
46 Ibid., p. 125.
47 *SR*, 20 Apr. 1847.
48 Cork City and County Archives, BG/69/A, *Cork Board of Guardians Minute Books, Book 10.* Minutes of 19 Jan. 1850.
49 CSORP, G:68057, 1850.
50 Ibid.

4. ALCOCK

1   Ronan O'Rahilly, *Benjamin Alcock, first professor of anatomy and physiology in Queen's College, Cork* (Cork, 1948), p. 14.
2   CSORP, 1853, 1996; Kane to Young, 24 Feb. 1853, p. 2.
3   Ibid.
4   Deborah Alcock, *Walking with God: a memoir of the Ven. J. Alcock, late archdeacon of Waterford* (London, 1887), p. 5.
5   Whately, *Poorer classes in Ireland,* Supp. Appendix B, Part I, p. 32.
6   *Report of the Poor Law Commissioners into the Medical Charities, Ireland* (Dublin, 1841), (324, 324a), xi, p. 68.
7   Alcock, *Walking with God*, p. 6.
8   The Apothecaries' Hall Dublin trained, examined and licensed apothecaries. It was established by Act of Parliament in 1791 (31 Geo. III). In 1837, the medical school of the Apothecaries' Hall was established in Cecilia Street, Dublin, which received the necessary recognition from the Royal College of Surgeons in Ireland.
9   *Apothecaries' Hall Minute Book, 1838–1849*, 26 Sept. 1838 and 25 Oct. 1838, University College Cork.
10 *SN*, 11 Nov. 1846.
11 Ibid., 15 Nov. 1846.
12 *AH Minute Book*, Agreement between the Governor and Company of Apothecaries' Hall and their Professors regarding the School of Medicine of the Hall, 19 May 1837.
13 Ibid., Alcock to Speedy, 16 Oct. 1849.
14 Ibid., Corbett to Speedy, 9 Oct. and 17 Oct. 1849.
15 Ibid., Speedy to Alcock, 9 Oct. 1849.
16 Ibid., Alcock to Speedy, 23 Oct. 1849.
17 Robert William Smith (1807–73), distinguished surgeon and founder of the Pathological Society of Dublin. See Davis Coakley, *Irish masters of medicine* (Dublin, 1992), pp 143–8.
18 *AH Minute Book*; Decision of Robert Smith and Philip Bevan, 2 Nov. 1849.
19 CSORP, 1853, 1996; Kane to Young, 24 Feb. 1853.
20 *AH Minute Book*; Speedy to Alcock, 27 Apr. 1847.
21 CSORP, 1853, 1996; Alcock to Kane, 11 Nov. 1851.
22 Alcock's printed gloss on Albani's letter as it appeared in his memorial.
23 A record of this notice does not exist in UCC archives but it deeply offended the College Council who judged it to be 'calculated to injure discipline in the College'.
24 CSORP, 1853, 1996; undated memo, probably written by Sir Thomas Larcom in February or March 1853. (See *Dictionary of Irish architects*, dia.ie, for further information about Larcom.)
25 CSORP, 1853, 1996; Kane to Young, 24 Feb. 1853.
26 Ibid., Belfour to Albani, 17 Jan. 1853.
27 Ibid., Hobart to Lord Lieutenant, 2 Mar. 1854.
28 CSORP, 1853, 1996; Alcock to Bullen.
29 CSORP, 1853, 1996; Bullen to Young, 17 Oct. 1853, enclosing the above.

30 CSORP, 1854, 13014; Alcock's memorial
  to the Earl of St Germans, Appendix F.
31 Ibid., Appendix G.
32 CSORP, 1853, 8; Bullen's return for
  quarter ended 31 Dec. 1852.
33 CSORP, 1854, 13014; Appendix H.
34 CSORP, 1853, 1996; memo probably
  written by Larcom in February or March
  1853. Alcock delayed filling the post
  until Humphries was qualified.
35 CSORP, 1853, 1996; a group of 3 letters
  tagged 11930. Gardiner to Alcock, 15
  Nov. 1852.
36 Ibid.
37 Ibid., Bullen to Young, 17 Oct. 1853.
38 CSORP, 1853, 1996; O'Connor to
  Bullen, 24 Oct. 1853.
39 Ibid.
40 CSORP, 1853, 1996; Alcock to Larcom,
  5 Dec. 1853.
41 Ibid., Alcock to Young, 14 Dec. 1853.
42 Ibid., Alcock to Young, 24 Dec. 1853.
43 Ibid.
44 Ibid.
45 Ibid., Kane to Larcom, 28 Dec. 1853.
46 Ibid., Alcock to Bullen, 6 Jan. 1854.
47 Ibid., Bullen to Albani, 7 Jan. 1854.
48 Ibid., Alcock to Young, 23 Jan. 1854.
49 Ibid., Bullen to Young, 22 Feb. 1854.
50 Ibid., Larcom to Alcock, 28 Feb. 1854.
51 Ibid., Alcock to Young, 14 Mar. 1854.
52 CSORP, 1855, 4494.
53 *SR*, 19 July 1855 and *DMP,* 8 Aug. 1855.
54 CSORP, 1858, 17228.
55 Hanna and Crowe, *What happened to
  Benjamin Alcock?*, pp 50–64.
56 Desmond MacHale, *The life and work of
  George Boole* (Cork, 2014).

5. CAESAR

1 Murphy, *The College*, p. 91. The inspector
  in charge of the investigation always called
  Caesar by the more colloquial 'Cosar'.
2 CSOOP, 1854, 61.
3 CSOOP, 1849, 124.
4 CSOOP, 1854, 61.
5 Ibid. ,
6 *SR*, 29 Oct. 1836.
7 *CC*, 11 Oct. 1842.
8 CSOOP, 1854, 61.
9 CSORP, H4845, 1850.
10 *CC*, 5 Dec. 1857.
11 Ibid.
12 *DMP*, 29 Jan. 1862, p. 128.
13 Ibid.
14 Minutes of Council of the Royal
  College of Surgeons of England, RCS-
  GOV/2/1/6, (X) 1854–1862. Courtesy of
  RCSE.
15 *CC*, 4 July 1864.
16 *CC*, 19 Oct. 1858.
17 Personal communication from the family
  of Dr Seaborne.
18 Murphy, *The College,* pp 82–94.
19 Sir John Pope Hennessy (1834–91),
  medical graduate of Queen's College
  from a Catholic land-owning family
  in Co. Cork who went on to have
  a distinguished career in the British
  colonial service becoming
  Governor-in-Chief of the Windward
  Islands (1873–7), Governor of Hong
  Kong (1877–82) and Governor of
  Mauritius (1883–9).
20 *CC*, 23 Feb. 1864.
21 Murphy, *The College*, p. 88.
22 Ibid., p. 86.
23 MacHale, *The life and work of George Boole*,
  p. 261.
24 *DMP*, 28 Dec. 1864, p. 644.
25 *CE*, 17 Mar. 1865.
26 *CE*, 29 Mar. 1865.
27 *CE*, 2 Apr. 1868.
28 *SR*, 4 Oct. 1865.
29 *SR*, 16 June 1864.
30 *CE,* 20 Sept. 1866.